# 《中国税务绩效管理》（中英文）

## 国家税务总局课题组

组　长：王　军

副组长：王道树

成　员：黄　运　付树林　刘尊涛　史　峰　荣海楼
　　　　宋　震　何　强　赵一静　谢自强　郑刚强

执　笔：何　强

翻　译：张　晨　蔡育新

# Performance Management in China State Taxation Administration
# ( Chinese–English Bilingual Version )

## The Research Group of the STA

Project Leader：Wang Jun

Deputy Project Leader：Wang Daoshu

Project Members：

Huang Yun　Fu Shulin　Liu Zuntao　Shi Feng
Rong Hailou　Song Zhen　He Qiang　Zhao Yijing
Xie Ziqiang　Zheng Gangqiang

Author：He Qiang

Translators：Zhang Chen　Cai Yuxin

Performance
Management **China**
in
State Taxation Administration

【中英文对照】

# 中国税务
# 绩效管理

国家税务总局课题组　著

人民出版社

# 目　录

/

**Contents**

## ▍ 中文部分
Chinese Section

## 英文部分
English Section

中文部分

党的十八大以来，税务总局党委深入学习贯彻习近平总书记关于"完善领导干部考核评价机制"①"沉下心来抓落实"② 等重要指示批示精神，按照新时代党的组织路线和中央关于"严格绩效管理"等部署要求，聚焦以"抓好党务、干好税务、带好队伍"为主要内容的新时代税收现代化建设总目标，围绕抓班子、带队伍、促落实、提质效，在全国税务系统全面推行横向到边、纵向到底、责任到岗、任务到人的绩效管理，助力税收现代化"蓝图变现实"取得积极成效。

习近平总书记指出，"坚持和发展中国特色社会主义，需要不断在实践和理论上进行探索、用发展着的理论指导发展着的实践。"③ 税务总局党委在实施绩效管理过程中，

---

① 《习近平谈治国理政》第三卷，外文出版社 2020 年版，第 50 页。

② 《习近平关于力戒形式主义官僚主义重要论述选编》，中央文献出版社 2020 年版，第 100 页。

③ 习近平：《在哲学社会科学工作座谈会上的讲话》，《人民日报》2016 年 5 月 19 日。

既注重实践创新、以实践深化理论，又注重理论提升、以理论指导实践，引起学术界和实务界的高度关注。2019年5月，中央宣传部全国哲学社会科学工作办公室将"推动高质量发展的税务绩效管理：实践发展与理论研究"确定为2019年度国家社会科学基金重大委托项目，赋予税务部门为推进国家治理现代化特别是政府绩效管理学科体系、学术体系、话语体系建设提供助益的重大责任。

税务总局党委和项目负责人王军局长高度重视课题研究及本书写作工作，充分调动税务系统内外的研究积极性，突出实践性、应用性、示范性、引领性，倾力把研究报告书写在奋进新时代的税收事业发展中。最终成果报告在介绍研究缘起、意义、现状、内容、方法的基础上，按照"为什么做""做什么""具体怎么做""以什么为保障""重点突破什么""做得怎么样""有什么启示和展望"的基本逻辑，对税务绩效管理近十年来的实践和理论创新进行深入梳理和系统阐述，主要内容概括为"四个方面"的实施背景、"一二三四五"的设计思路、"五个环节"的运行过程、"四个强化"的支撑保障、实现"三个重点突破"、发挥出"四个积极效应"、得出"十条管理启示"、提出"五方面未来展望"。

*Chapter*

# 关于"税务绩效管理的实施背景"

党的十八大以来，税务总局党委立足于适应全面深化改革大势、服务经济社会发展大局、带好税务系统大队伍，持续推进和深化绩效管理，实施背景概括起来就是中央有要求、税务有需求、条件有优势、实践有借鉴。

## （一）实施税务绩效管理是践行"两个维护"的实际行动

税务总局党委牢记习近平总书记对带好税务系统干部队伍的殷切嘱托，对标对表新时代党的组织路线，认真落实中央关于健全干部考核评价体系、严格绩效管理的部署要求，为确保全国税务系统听党指挥、担当作为，心往一处想、劲往一处使，探索和实施税务绩效管理。

## （二）实施税务绩效管理是推动税收改革发展的有力抓手

税务总局党委着眼新时代赋予税务部门光荣艰巨的使命任务，为推动"抓好党务"加强党对税收工作的全面领导、推动"干好税务"充分发挥税收职能作用、推动"带好队伍"倾情打造税务铁军，确保贯彻落实好习近平总书记关于税收工作的重要指示批示精神和中央关于税收改革发展的重大决策部署，探索和实施税务绩效管理。

## （三）实施税务绩效管理是契合税务系统优势的科学之选

税务总局党委立足全国税务系统从总局到省、市、县、乡税务机构具有垂直化的体制优势，抓好党务、干好税务、带好队伍具有同质化的业务优势，持续完善党的建设、税费服务、征收管理、内控监督等方面制度、规则和标准厚植规范化的工作优势，主动适应数字化时代加快金税工程建设打造信息化的技术优势，实事求是利用好税务系统现实条件，与时俱进把握好税收事业未来发展，经过深入调研、反复论证、集体决策、广泛动员，探索和实施税务绩效管理。

## （四）实施税务绩效管理是借鉴各方实践经验的创新之举

税务总局党委坚持开阔视野、广泛借鉴，从有关部门和地方的前期实践、古代中国政绩考核传统文化和外国政府及其税务部门做法中汲取有益经验，并针对一些单位在推行绩效管理中面临的问题，寻求创新求变的突破口，探索和实施税务绩效管理。

# 关于"税务绩效管理的设计思路"

政府绩效管理是推进国家治理现代化、构建政府治理体系的重要举措。税务绩效管理坚持以习近平新时代中国特色社会主义思想为指导，认真贯彻习近平总书记关于税收工作和完善干部考核评价体系、加强绩效考核等重要论述，致力于打造富于税务特色、具有典型效应、务实有效管用、突出创新引领的绩效管理模式，设计思路概括起来就是树立"一大战略导向"、构建"双轮驱动体系"、把握"三项实施原则"、运用"四个基础理论"、突出"五条内在机理"。

## （一）树立"一大战略导向"

税务总局党委深刻领悟习近平总书记关于"战略是从

全局、长远、大势上作出判断和决策"①等重要指示精神，锚定新时代税收现代化战略目标，以绩效管理促进全国税务系统上下同欲、勠力同心。一是着眼"提站位、扬优势"谋划战略。坚持继承与发展相结合，紧扣"提升站位、依法治税、深化改革、倾情带队"描绘税收现代化蓝图，确立税收现代化建设路线图、任务书。二是着眼"找差距、补短板"完善战略。坚持目标导向与问题导向相结合，紧扣"抓好党务、干好税务、带好队伍"，实事求是总结成绩，自觉主动查找差距，顺时应势不断推出升级版税收现代化战略并相应优化完善绩效管理体系。三是着眼"谱新篇、呈递进"落实战略。坚持抓常与抓长相结合，紧扣绩效指标一抓到底，既打基础又利长远，既推一域又促全局，化战略为行动，前后接续谱写税收现代化新篇章。

## （二）构建"双轮驱动体系"

按照中共中央办公厅印发的《党政领导干部考核工作条例》和中央组织部关于改进推动高质量发展政绩考核、开展公务员绩效管理试点工作等要求，税务绩效管理框架

---

① 《习近平谈治国理政》第四卷，外文出版社 2022 年版，第 31 页。

体系由侧重于"考核班子"的组织绩效和侧重于"评价干部"的个人绩效共同构成。一是构建组织绩效管理"4+4+4+N"框架体系。考评范围覆盖税务总局机关各司局，各省、自治区、直辖市和计划单列市税务局，税务总局驻各地特派员办事处和副省级城市税务局"四类对象"；指标内容归纳为党的全面领导、税收改革发展、工作运转保障、各方多维评价"四大板块"；指标考点基于年初工作部署、全国"两会"精神、年中新增任务、其他调整事项"四处来源"，并对需要啃的"硬骨头"工作实行"N个专项考评"。二是构建个人绩效管理"1+4+1"框架体系。夯实职业基础"一个基础"；立起平时考核、公认评价、业务能力、领导胜任力"四个支柱"；盖上数字人事数据应用"一个顶子"。组织绩效管理像"车头"，以抓班子发挥牵引带动作用；个人绩效管理像"车身"，以管干部实现整体推动效果。

## （三）把握"三项实施原则"

切实遵循推进改革创新的基本规律和策略，充分认识绩效管理既是先进管理工具又是"世界性难题"，牢牢把握"三个坚定不移"的实施原则，坚决做到善始善终、善

作善成。一是坚定不移地推。从 2014 年起，确定"一年
试运行、两年见成效、三年创品牌、在此基础上再接再厉
开创新局面"的绩效管理总布局，步步为营，年年有成，
积小胜为大胜。二是坚定不移地改。彰显持续改进的绩效
管理核心要义，先立后破、不破不立，固根基、扬优势、
补短板、强弱项，以自我革命的精神不断优化完善基本框
架、绩效指标和考评规则，一年一升级，累计升级 10 个
版本，促进绩效管理制度机制体系更加成熟定型。三是坚
定不移地用。以"绩效管理不用则废"的强烈意识，切实
把绩效考评结果运用作为绩效管理的"生命线"，顶住压
力用、拓展渠道用、公道合理用，在与干部任用、年度考
核、人才培养、评先评优等挂钩运用中强化绩效意识、倒
逼绩效改进、促进绩效扎根。

## （四）运用"四个基础理论"

坚持理论的价值在于指导实践，结合实际创造性运用
现代管理基础理论，为税务绩效管理的战略谋划、目标分
解、执行落实、过程控制以及组织绩效与个人绩效有机衔
接等提供重要指导。一是战略管理理论。依据该理论立足
组织长远发展方向、制定战略规划并采取措施推动实施的

核心观点，围绕税收现代化战略，突出全局性、长远性和根本性，引导各级税务机关和广大税务干部既立足当前又面向未来，既抬头看路又埋头苦干。二是目标管理理论。依据该理论将长远战略转化为年度计划并设置绩效指标、明确责任分工的核心观点，强调岗位就是责任、团结就是力量，把税收工作年度重点任务目标逐级逐层分解并压实到单位、部门和个人，共促战略目标实现。三是全面质量管理理论。依据该理论对落实任务实行全过程质量控制（PDCA循环）的核心观点，通过打造"战略—目标—执行—考评—奖惩—改进"的税务绩效管理完整链条，首尾相顾、连环驱动、螺旋上升，形成一个确保税收工作高质量发展的良性循环。四是组织行为学理论。依据该理论注重从心理学、生理学、社会学等层面研究组织发展的核心观点，坚持以人为本，注重人文关怀，关注心理健康，结合深入细致开展思想政治工作、科学合理配置人力资源，促进持续改善干部绩效，实现个人成长和组织发展的共进。

## （五）突出"五条内在机理"

深入挖掘税务绩效管理发挥积极作用的原理和"门

道"，精心设置相互联系、相互促进、"牵一发而动全身"的规则和机制。一是压实责任、传导压力"抓落实"。基于贯彻中央"严格绩效管理，突出责任落实，确保权责一致"的部署要求，通过健全"横向到边、纵向到底、责任到岗、任务到人"的绩效管理格局，促进系统上下层层传导压力、人人激发活力，打造明责、聚力、狠抓落实的管理体系。二是环环相扣、持续优化"强撬动"。基于着力形成"环环相扣、压茬推进"的管理闭环，强调将"年度有计划、计划有落实、落实有评价、评价有奖惩、奖惩有推进"的组织绩效管理"五有"和"干部管理日常化、日常管理指标化、指标管理数字化、数字管理累积化、累积管理可比化、可比管理挂钩化、挂钩管理导向化"的个人绩效管理"七化"匹配起来，打造衔接、优化、关联撬动的管理体系。三是多元考核、多维评价"精画像"。基于管理本身是一种平衡的艺术，不同考核主体有可能"横看成岭侧成峰"，不同评价维度可能"远近高低各不同"，引入平衡计分卡（BSC），注重统筹上下左右内外的考评主体和时间、数量、质量、效果的考评维度，打造立体、持续、综合平衡的管理体系。四是激励约束、激发活力"促提升"。基于调动积极性、强化自驱力，以正向激励为主深化绩效考评结果运用，形成潜移默化的激励鞭策，促使"人人讲绩效、事事求绩效""后进赶先进、一起向前进"，打造激励、鞭策、向上向善的管理体系。五是层级联动、内外互动"重协同"。基于以税务总局为主、与省区市党委和政府实行双重领导的管理体制，着眼构建税收共治格局、提高税法遵从度和社会满意度，统筹税务系统考评和地方党政考评、机关考评和基层考评、纳税人缴费人和税务人评价等各个方面，打造开放、贯通、协同共进的管理体系。

# 关于"税务绩效管理的运行过程"

根据中央关于"优化行政决策、行政执行、行政组织、行政监督体制"的精神，税务绩效管理融入税务行政管理过程，与税收工作的决策、执行、组织、监督一体推进，运行过程概括起来就是"五个环节"，具体包括科学编制绩效指标、扎实推进绩效执行、有序开展绩效考评、深化运用考评结果、着力抓好绩效改进。

## （一）科学编制绩效指标

主要是"四定"：一是厘定编制流程。按照"研提指标编制思路—细化初拟考评指标—多轮沟通逐一完善—集思广益征求意见—民主集中审定发布"的流程编制绩效指标。二是设定指标内容。坚持把贯彻落实习近平总书记重要指示批示精神和党中央、国务院决策部署，服务高质量发展、推动税收现代化的目标任务等，作为设置指标内容的基本依据，为各级税务机关设定彰显中国之治、体现税务特色、凸显战略目标、涵盖重点任务的组织绩效指标体系；坚持政治统领，围绕德、能、勤、绩、廉，根据不同岗位的差异性，突出组织绩效与个人绩效有机衔接，为每名税务干部设定适应组织愿景、适配岗位职责、适合自身实际、适于团队协作的个人绩效指标体系。三是确定考评标准。从税收工作的实际出发，明确时间标准，严格质量标准，突出效果标准，虑今顾远设置"跳一跳、够得着"的目标值，防止过高或过低、过繁或过简，最大限度做到可实现、可控制、可衡量，使每个单位、每位干部对做什么、怎么做、做到什么程度、什么时限完成清晰明了。四是赋定分值权重。税务组织绩效考评按千分制赋值，个人绩效考评按百分制赋值，并根据每一项指标所属类别、任务量的大小、完成的难易程度以及特定的管理要求等因素确定在整个指标体系中所占的分值权重。税务总局编制考评机关司局、省税务局、驻各地特派办、副省级城市税务局绩效指标，下一级单位分别根据上级指标，结合实际编制考评下级单位和机关内设部门指标，纵向上总局考评省

局、省局考评市局、市局考评县局、县局考评分局，横向
上总局机关考评司局、省局机关考评处室、市县局机关考
评科（股）室，并向每个岗位、每位干部延伸编制个人绩
效指标，就像打通人的脉络神经，实现"如身使臂，如臂
使指"的管理效果。

## （二）扎实推进绩效执行

主要是"四抓"：一是"责任到岗、任务到人"抓承
接分解。围绕聚焦工作重点不折不扣推进绩效执行，凸显
"指标分下去、责任扛起来"，做到"千斤重担众人挑、人
人肩上有指标"。在组织绩效方面，对考评内容相对单一
的指标，根据职能确定具体落实部门；对综合性指标的承
接分解，根据实际情况明确牵头部门和配合部门。在个人
绩效方面，依托完备的岗责体系，将组织绩效指标分解到
岗到人，实现"组织绩效指标—部门绩效指标—个人绩效
指标—具体责任人员"的递次关联，让每名干部的个人
绩效"小目标"都来源并服务于组织绩效"大目标"。二
是"上下左右、考前考后"抓沟通辅导。围绕抓住工作要
点有的放矢推进绩效执行，凸显"沟通要畅通、辅导加引
导"，做到"心中有数、眼里有活、脚下有路"。考评者与

被考评者，紧扣绩效计划、指标执行、分析改进等，将沟通辅导贯穿于绩效管理全过程，上级指点督促有引导，同级交流借鉴有疏导，考前研提落实任务良策，考后商定绩效改进良方，多轮沟通开胸顺气、多措并举提质增效。正如税务干部从实践中体悟到的："无论定指标，还是严考评；无论搞分析，还是明奖惩，都离不开沟通。只有将沟通融入绩效管理各个环节，才能真正让各方心脉相连、心气相通。"三是"对标对表、查短扬长"抓分析讲评。围绕切中工作弱点扬长补短推进绩效执行，凸显"对标对表分析、知短知弱讲评"，做到"知差距而弥补，知不足而奋进"。组织绩效与个人绩效压茬推进，逐级逐层逐个开展绩效讲评，突出"讲实"，既讲原理又讲原因；突出"评好"，既评标杆又评标兵；突出"查短"，既要揭短又不护短，增强持续改进压力和比学赶超动力。四是"全链条督、多维度促"抓过程监控。围绕打通工作堵点保质保量推进绩效执行，凸显"全过程监控、动态化跟进"，做到"及时纠偏，即知即改"。坚持事有人干、干有人督、督有人考，适时采集相关信息数据，随时监测指标执行进展，及时发现各维度存在问题，加强过程质量监控，确保"不脱节、不偏向、不失速"。

## （三）有序开展绩效考评

主要是"四考"：一是明确考评主体。各级税务机关绩效考评主体是各级税务局党委，由相应领导和职能部门具体实施。对个人绩效，根据公务员相互之间的关联度、知情度，按照层次关系确定考评的具体实施者。二是优化考评方法。根据绩效指标不同属性，相应匹配直接扣分法、基准加减法、排序得分法、分档计分法、量化计分法、前沿距离法等，力求方法得当、考评得力、结果得宜。三是严格考评程序。组织绩效考评按照考前提醒、被考评单位填报、考评单位审核、绩效办复核、成绩审定、成绩发布、成绩反馈、核查评议、争议处理等环节开展；个人绩效考核以平时考核为重点，以按周记实、按季考评、按年累计的方式，及时记录和考核日常工作、德才表现等各方面情况。四是严肃考评纪律。考评者不得搞形式、走过场，不得泄露测评结果等考评工作秘密，不得借考评之机谋取私利；被考评者不得弄虚作假，不得干扰、妨碍考评工作。

## （四）深入运用考评结果

主要是"四挂钩一拓宽"：一是与选拔任用挂钩。深入贯彻落实《党政领导干部选拔任用工作条例》《关于进一步激励广大干部新时代新担当新作为的意见》等制度规定，将绩效考评结果与干部选拔任用相挂钩，通过对选拔任用干部增减晋升名额，对干部晋升职务职级设立绩效条件，旗帜鲜明树立重实干重实绩的用人导向，激励广大税务干部以更加奋发有为的状态履职尽责、开拓进取，争创一流业绩。2015 年至 2022 年，因年度组织绩效考评排名前两位或进步最快，在总职数内累计对机关司局增加 19 个司局级和处级职务（或相应职级）晋升名额；对省局增加 14 个司局级职务（或相应职级）晋升名额；对派出机构增加 2 个处级职务（或相应职级）晋升名额。2019 年至 2022 年，税务系统共有 4689 名干部因考核排名末位不予晋升职级，且在选拔任用时暂不予考虑；344 名试用期干部因个人数字人事年度考核得分排名末位（2021 年起，改为排名后 20%）延期转正考核。2020 年，税务总局机关 1 名司局长因该司局连续两年绩效考核排名末位，按照绩效结果运用办法规定，被调整到其他单位担任二把手。

2019 年税务系统副厅局级领导干部选任工作中，有两个省级局党委推荐的本地任职建议人选，因个人绩效成绩连续两年均为 2 段，不符合税务总局相关要求，未予同意。2017 年至 2022 年，共有 1 名司局级干部，12 名处级干部因当年绩效考评成绩排名末位，延期办理试用期转正。2020 年税务系统优秀年轻干部调研工作中，税务总局机关 1 名副司长、1 名处长，税务系统 3 名副厅局级领导干部，因个人绩效不符合要求未列入优秀年轻干部名单。2022 年，税务系统晋升各级领导职务的干部共 15344 名，全部符合数字人事年度考核得分近两年均位于第 2 段以上且其中一年位于第 1 段的要求。二是与年度考核挂钩。深入贯彻公务员法及配套法规，将绩效考评结果作为公务员年度考核的重要参考，并在公务员考核政策范围内将"优秀"等次名额与组织绩效考评结果挂钩。2015 年至 2022 年，因年度组织绩效考评排名前列或进步较快，累计对机关司局增加了 16 个公务员年度考核优秀名额，对省税务局增加了 16 个班子成员年度考核优秀名额，对派出机构增加了 2 个公务员年度考核优秀名额；同时，相应减少排名靠后或退步较多单位的优秀名额。2019 年至 2022 年，税务系统累计对 8424 个单位（部门）增加了 13907 名公务员年度考核优秀名额，对 333 名干部确定为"基本称职"和"不称职"；税务总局机关累计确定公务员年度考核优秀 695 人次，全部位于个人绩效年度考核第 1 段。2020 年至 2022 年，报经中央公务员主管部门审批同意，根据组织绩效年度考核结果，累计对 26 个机关司局、37 个省税务局、3 个派出机构提高了公务员年度考核优秀比例。税务系统累计对 8094 个单位（部门）提高了公务员年度考核优秀等次比例。三是与人才培养挂钩。围绕实施人才兴税战略，把税务人才的选拔、培育、使用、管理等纳入绩效考评体系，并制定《税务领军人才培养专项绩效考评办法》，形成上下联动、齐抓共管的良好局面。同时参考个人绩效数据加强干部教育培养，按照"缺什么补什么"的原则，对干部进行培训培养、调学调训、安排实践锻炼，补齐能力素质短板。近年来，领军人才到税务总局先后有 372 人次直接参与国税地税征管体制改革工作，191 人次直接参与个人所得税改革、发票电子化改革等重大攻坚任务，近 2000 人次参加专项工作，充分发挥"敢担当、善引领、贵恒进"的重要作用，人才示范效应明显，系统上下高度认可。同时，从已结业的领军人才中选择绩效成绩优异、综合素质突出、外语水平较高、发展潜力较大的优秀处级以上干部，送到我驻外使领馆、国际组织锻炼或国外大学深造1—2年，拓展其国际视野，回国后放在改革开放前沿地区税务局重用。相关人员在各自岗位上得到充分认可，如经济合作与发展组织（OECD）秘书处认为，中国税务部门派遣的税务官员专业能力和敬业精神都很过硬。同时，创新建立"学测用评"制度体系，将干部学习情况与绩效考核有机结合起来，引导全系统干部在日常学、日常练中加强政治理论和税收业务学习。截至2022年底，全系统共培养战略人才、领军人才、专业骨干、岗位能手等各类人才6万余人，人才总量与2017年相比增加近2倍，占全系统在职干部8.7%，人才引领示范效应愈发显现。2022年，各省税务局从基层税务机关累计遴选干部440名，全部符合数字人事年度考核得分近两年均位于第2段以上的要求；其中，因上两年数字人事年度考核均位于第1段，符合优先考虑的干部占比52%。四是与评先评优挂钩。单位和个人评先评优必看绩效成绩，对组织绩效突出的单位，适当增加评先评优的相关名额；干部评先评优，个人绩效必须符合相应条件。2019年至2022年，税务系统累计有20个单位获评国家级先进集体，1608个单位获评省部级先进集体，均为绩效优秀单位；有

56 人次获得国家级先进个人表彰，1538 人次获得省部级
先进个人表彰，个人绩效考评均成绩排名前列；税务总局
机关共评选出 220 名优秀共产党员和 40 名优秀党务工作
者，个人绩效考评成绩均排名前列。五是拓宽运用渠道。
结合追责问责"拧紧弦"，以绩效数据为重要参考推进领
导干部能上能下或者对干部进行问责。2019 年至 2022 年，
因年度绩效考评连续两年排名末两位，税务系统累计对
73 个单位（部门）的主要负责人予以调整；并根据数字人
事年度考核和平时考核结果，累计对 194 名不担当、不作
为的干部进行调整处理。注重人文关怀"强信心"，充分
发挥绩效辅导沟通作用，扎实做好思想政治和人文关怀工
作，不断增强税务干部的获得感、认同感和归属感。2019
年至 2022 年，累计对干部推送"政治生日"及其他节日
祝福 736 万人次，累计对 38.35 万名干部颁发了终身奉献
税收事业荣誉证书。强化持续激励"防躺平"，统筹考虑
连续年度因素，综合运用当年和前两年考评结果，对绩效
优秀单位适当提高数字人事年度考核第 1 段人员比例，连
续两年均被确定为绩效优秀单位的再提高一定比例，引导
进步者更优秀，鞭策退步者迎头赶上，促进从"一马当先"
到"万马奔腾"。2019 年至 2022 年，根据组织绩效年度

考评结果，税务总局累计对确定为绩效优秀单位的 40 个
机关司局、55 个省税务局、6 个派出机构提高了个人绩效
年度考核第 1 段的比例（当年确定为绩效优秀单位的，提
高 5%；连续 2 年确定为绩效优秀单位的，提高 10%；下
同）。2021 年，根据组织绩效年度考评结果，税务系统累
计对确定为绩效优秀单位的 12296 个单位（部门）提高了
数字人事年度考核第 1 段的比例。

## （五）着力抓好绩效改进

主要是"三及时一共同"：一是考评者及时向被考评
者反馈考评结果。组织绩效按月向被考评单位"点对点"
反馈考评成绩、考评明细和存在不足，帮助其改进提升；
按季度向所有被考评单位公布考评结果，促进互比互鉴。
个人绩效通过信息系统及时向干部本人推送分析报告，并
可查看同级同类干部的最高分、平均分、中位值，主管领
导通过工作点评、个别谈话等方式，帮助干部找准坐标位
置，明确前进方向和改进措施。二是考评者与被考评者及
时会诊问题短板。建立完善"评价—分析—改进—再评
价"的改进机制，针对考评结果及时分析问题短板和失分
原因，由考评者对考评成绩较低的被考评者，提示指出哪

项工作出了问题、有什么改进建议，并听取被考评者的意见，共同商定绩效改进的方向、重点和措施。三是被考评者及时制定可操作的改进方案。因事因人制定绩效改进的行动方案，并打通组织绩效与个人绩效，从大处着眼，从细节入手，一点一滴地优化完善，以求组织与个人"双改进、双提升"。四是考评者与被考评者共同推动改进提升。通过提升思想认识、优化指标设置、加强执行监控，机关与基层、上级与下级共同推进工作持续提升。具体实践中，各单位以指标考评标准为导向，既分析"如何落实"，又分析"落实得怎样"，把诊断出的"问题"及时纳入到下一环节的考评中。有的通过内部讲评、风险排查、督办反馈等方式，促进工作持续改进；有的见微知著，针对考评被扣分的情况，从改进工作角度强化"分小事大"意识，积极完善制度机制；有的以点带面，抓重点难点，发挥关键指标的带动作用；有的举一反三，进一步细化目标任务，明确工作措施，不断提升工作质效。

# 关于"税务绩效管理的支撑保障"

税务绩效管理依靠组织、制度、技术的变革，强化支撑保障，不断优化完善，同时以海纳百川的眼界胸怀争取各方助力，概括起来就是"四个强化"。

## （一）强化组织领导

一是党委统一领导。各级税务局党委加强对绩效管理工作的组织领导，"一把手"负总责，班子成员分工负责，定期听取工作汇报，研究决定重大事项。二是绩效管理工作领导小组统筹。各级税务机关在党委统一领导下，成立绩效管理工作领导小组，主要负责人任组长，相关负责人任副组长，有关部门负责人为成员，负责统筹部署和指导绩效管理工作，审定绩效管理发展规划和制度办法、绩效计划、绩效指标和考评规则、绩效考评结果等。三是绩效管理工作领导小组办公室协调。领导小组办公室在税务总局按组织绩效与个人绩效两大块分设在办公厅、人事司。省、市税务局绩效办设在考核考评部门，县税务局设在办公室，负责绩效管理日常工作。四是考核考评部门专司其职。税务总局办公厅设立具体承担组织绩效管理工作的绩效管理处，个人绩效管理由人事司公务员管理处具体承担。2018 年机构改革后，在机构编制总体压缩的情况下，省、市税务机关成立专职考核考评部门，专司编制绩效指标、开展绩效考评、抓好绩效改进等方面具体工作。五是绩效管理专职队伍主动担当。各级税务机关配齐配强绩效管理专职队伍，并在全系统各层级建立以绩效专干为主、绩效联络员为辅的绩效管理干部队伍。六是各级各部门和广大干部积极参与。在绩效管理链条中，各级税务机关及其内设部门都有可能承担考评职责，成为考评者，同时均承担指标工作任务，从而成为被考评者。各层级各部门各岗位全面融入、积极参与。七是绩效考评委员会民主评议。绩效考评注重全过程民主。绩效考评委员会在领导小组领导下开展工作，负责对绩效管理重大事项的审议和裁定，包括开展评议核查、分析评估绩效管理运行情况、提出改进意见、审议绩效考评中的争议事项以及对被考评单位申诉提出处理意见等。

## （二）强化制度保障

一是持续完善制度体系。组织绩效管理建立"1+2+4"制度体系，即"一份指导意见"：《国家税务总局关于实施绩效管理的意见》；"两个具体办法"：《全国税务系统绩效管理办法》《绩效考评结果运用办法》；"四套考评规则"：对机关司局、对省税务局、对驻各地特派办、对副省级城市税务局年度绩效考评规则。个人绩效管理建立"1+9"制度体系，即"一个总办法"：《税务系统数字人事实施办法》；"九个子办法"：《干部平时考核实施办法》《数字人事量化计分规则》《个人绩效管理指标编制指引》《税务系统新录用公务员初任培训管理办法》《外部评价管理办法》《业务能力升级管理办法》《领导胜任力测试管理办法》《数字人事结果运用办法》《深化数字人事数据应用工作指导意见》。二是持续增进制度认同。按照税务总局党委统一部署，各级税务机关结合本地实际，通过讲明绩效原理、讲清绩效规定、讲透绩效疑难、讲好绩效故事，引导广大税务干部主动认知、自觉躬行，理解实施绩效管理的重要意义，掌握实施路径和破解疑难问题的具体办法，既"知其然"又"知其所以然"，在见人见事见效中不断加深对"人人为绩效、绩效为人人"的认同。三是持续深化制度执行。通过各级领导带动执行、嵌入流程撬动执行、督导跟进推动执行，以"吆喝百遍不如较真一次"的鲜明态度，维护绩效管理制度的权威性，促进制度遵从。四是持续加强制度评估。紧密联系绩效管理运行实际，既"以下评上"又"以外评内"，对制度执行情况进行跟踪评估问效，促进不断优化、执行有效。

## （三）强化技术支撑

一是绩效管理与金税工程建设互促共进。既依托金税工程建设提升绩效管理信息化水平，使绩效管理有数据可取、有痕迹可查，加大机生机汇机考力度，为提升绩效管理水平赋能；又通过绩效管理推进金税工程建设，将全面上线并平稳运行金税三期核心应用系统、信息系统整合优化、建成自然人税收管理信息系统、搭建全国最大的政务专有云平台、推进智慧税务建设等纳入绩效考评，确保落实落地。二是健全绩效管理信息系统。适应税务绩效管理发展先后升级推出三个版本，逐步完善量化计分考评、机生机汇考评、360°测评、多维度分析报告、考评结果查询、数字人事信息推送等功能模块，充分满足绩效管理运行需求。三是深化各个系统互联互通。税务绩效管理信息系统通过接口设置，实现与税收管理服务、决策分析、内控监督、统计核算以及党建、公文、外部第三方评价、征信等系统的衔接，夯实自动化考评基础。四是推进绩效管理智能化升级。各类绩效指标不同程度都有相应信息系统作为考评数据来源。适应税收数字化升级和智能化改造进程，逐步实现对组织和个人绩效自动化考评。

## （四）强化各方助力

从起步阶段论证设计绩效管理制度框架，到正式实施阶段推进绩效管理优化升级，主动听取专家学者和外部门同行意见，强化对税务绩效管理运行全过程的助力推动作用。一是助力绩效管理决策。邀请专家学者参与绩效管理可行性论证和制度体系设计。每年召开由专家学者、企业与新闻媒体代表参加的专题研讨会，为完善框架体系、科学编制绩效指标和考评规则等提出宝贵意见。二是助力绩效管理运行。邀请专家担任绩效考评委员会委员，参与绩效指标、考评结果、争议事项等审核裁定工作，发挥专家学者专业性更强、评判更具客观性的优势。三是助力绩效管理培训。每年举办绩效管理师资培训班，邀请绩效管理实务界和理论界专家学者授课，帮助培养税务绩效管理专业骨干力量。四是助力绩效管理研究。通过联合成立课题组等方式，与有关专家学者加强合作，深入研究税务绩效管理制度机制、指标体系、结果运用、绩效文化等，形成一系列研究成果，营造实践、研究、再实践、再研究的浓厚氛围。

# 关于"税务绩效管理的重点突破"

税务总局党委深入贯彻习近平总书记关于"打硬仗，啃硬骨头，确保干一件成一件"①的重要指示精神，针对党政部门特别是税务部门自身抓班子、管干部、严考评面临的"慢性病""常见病"乃至"顽瘴痼疾"，想方设法觅求破解之策，精益求精完善制度机制，使税务绩效管理针对性、科学性和实效性得到持续提升。

## （一）想方设法破解"严抓班子"面临的难题

抓好班子，才能带好队伍、促好落实。破解严抓班子面临的难题，是税务绩效管理的首要任务。一是破解上级

---

① 《对标重要领域和关键环节改革 继续啃硬骨头确保干一件成一件》，《人民日报》2019 年 1 月 24 日。

抓下级班子"不易抓"的难题。针对税务系统层级多、分布广、战线长，上级班子直接抓下级班子存在不小难度的状况，依据持续完善的税收现代化战略目标，进一步明确各年度工作主攻方向和着力点，凝聚起各级税务机关领导班子同心同向奋进的精气神。二是破解班长抓本级班子成员"不好抓"的难题。针对各级领导班子朝夕相处，班长抓班子成员可能抹不开面子的问题，将绩效管理从组织延伸至个人，实行班长个人绩效与本单位组织绩效全面挂钩，班子成员个人绩效与本单位和分管部门、下一级联系单位组织绩效挂钩，促进班长当好"第一责任人"、班子成员既抓好分管部门又推动全局工作。三是破解各层级班子"不齐抓"的难题。针对工作部署从税务总局到基层一线，如果中间环节动力和压力递减，则很难确保落实到位的问题，通过逐级分解指标、逐层压实责任、逐项开展考评，既在税务总局层面明确每项指标的考评司局，又在省、市、县税务局层面明确承接相关指标的责任领导，确保上下齐心协力、确保任务落实。四是破解以往只在年终考评班子"不常抓"的难题。针对过去对班子一年一考评，属于事后考，缺乏事前、事中监管，不利于过程控管、及时纠偏的问题，对绩效指标从数量、质量、进度、效果等

维度确定考评标准，按月、季、半年、全年实施考评，并
建立健全督查督办和绩效考评联动的"督考合一"机制，
事前定标准、事中有提醒、事后严考评，形成抓常抓细抓
长的常态化抓班子机制。五是破解抓班子奖惩措施有限
"不硬抓"的难题。针对过去考核对抓班子的成效缺乏激
励约束手段，导致不愿实打实、不敢硬碰硬、不争好上好
的问题，将绩效考评结果与干部任用、评先评优、公务员
年度考核挂钩，与推进领导干部能上能下、职务职级并行
相结合，确保考实用好，促进能者上、优者奖、庸者让。
六是破解抓班子有时主观能动性不足"不长抓"的难题。
针对以往管理易出现"推一推动一动，不推不动""抓一
时易、时时抓难"的问题，注重通过持续推进绩效管理、
持之以恒培育绩效文化，将加强价值认同、弘扬优良作风
与绩效管理融会贯通，积极引导各级税务局领导班子牢固
树立正确的政绩观，增强担当作为的自觉性和主动性。税
务绩效管理通过"抓班子"促进"班子抓"，推动一把手
抓一把手、上级班子抓下级班子、班长抓班子成员、班子
成员抓分管部门及联系单位更有章法，带动广大税务干部
干事创业、追求卓越。越来越多的领导干部越来越深刻地
认识到推行绩效管理的重要意义，少数之前有观望乃至抵

触心态的干部，也变成了积极参与者，不再纠结于搞不搞绩效管理，而是把注意力放在如何把绩效管理搞得更好上，实现从"要我搞"到"我要搞"的飞跃。有的领导干部对绩效管理从刚开始认为"次要"，到中间发现"重要"，现在成为"必要"；刚开始把绩效管理作为新增工作，甚至认为增加工作负担，现在感觉如影随形、习惯成自然，不讲绩效反而有些不适应。这是一个从"我干大家看"到"我干大家跟"再到"我干大家帮""我带大家干"的优化升级。

## （二）想方设法破解"严管干部"面临的难题

一是破解"知事不深、识人不准"的难题。个人绩效考核评价指标涵盖"一个基础、四个支柱"，形成既看发展又看基础，既看显绩又看潜绩的干部考核评价体系，努力为每位干部精准"画像"，提高考察和识别干部的精准度。二是破解"平时不算账、年终糊涂账"的难题。每名干部的平时考核成绩由组织绩效挂钩得分、个人绩效得分、领导评鉴得分、现实表现测评得分等构成。尤其是通过设立即时性考核指标，采取"按周记实、按季考评、按年归集"的方式计入干部"个人成长账户"，做到"一本平时账、工作全计量，好坏一眼望、庸懒无处藏"，引导干部"把功夫下在平时"。三是破解"一刀切、一锅煮"的难题。根据职务层级将人员分为领导班子正职、副职，部门正职、副职，其他人员5类，分别进行考核评价；结合公务员分类管理要求，建立干部业务能力评价体系，分为综合管理、纳税服务、征收管理、税务稽查和信息技术5类11级，并逐类逐级设置升级标准，定级情况计入"个人成长账户"，增强考核的针对性，避免"上下一般粗、左右一个样"。四是破解"干多干少、干好干坏一个样"的难题。在对干部考核评价指标进行量化的基础上，通过连续记录干部职业生涯各阶段的指标数据，时时累积、次次累积、年年累积，形成干部成长轨迹的"全息影像"，让愿干事、会干事、干成事者脱颖而出并受到褒奖和鼓励，让慢作为、不作为、乱作为者无法遁形并受到警醒和惩戒，引导各级领导干部更好忠于职守、担当奉献。五是破解"重考核评价、轻改进提升"的难题。根据组织绩效任务、年度重点任务、专项工作任务、领导交办任务等，编制个人绩效指标，及时开展考核评价和结果反馈，并通过以事察人、知事识人，更加准确地把脉问诊，促进广大税务干部自我改进、自我完善、自我提升。六是破解"论资排辈、平衡照顾"的难题。根据"个人成长账户"中记录的考核成绩，每年对干部考核结果分段进行综合排名。在评先评优、干部选拔任用、职务与职级并行中，优先考虑考核成绩排在第 1 段的干部；对考核成绩连续两年排在末位的，由党委研究，可作为不适宜担任现职的干部予以调整。通过个人数据的积累，既有利于识准用准好干部，也为问责处理不敢担当、不负责任、庸懒散拖的干部提供依据。广大税务干部切身感受到，对绩效管理经历了一个从"入眼"到"入脑"再到"入心"，从"相识"到"相知"再到"相守"的过程，干工作有了劲头、争上游有了奔头，热情更高了、动力更足了。

## （三）想方设法破解"严实考评"面临的难题

一是破解"政治素质不容易考核评价"的难题。围绕加强党对税收工作的全面领导，以政治标准作为硬杠杠设置组织绩效指标，同时制定 20 项干部政治表现负面清单，发生其中所列行为即在平时考评和年底划段中"一票否决"，使政治标准成为各级税务机关和广大税务干部履职尽责的"定盘星"。注重以"行"鉴"心"，把贯彻落实习近平总书记重要指示批示精神和党中央决策部署，贯彻新发展理念、推动高质量发展的实际表现和工作实绩，作为设置绩效指标、开展绩效考评的基本依据，作为检验政治素质的重要尺度，引导各级税务机关和广大税务干部以推动高质量发展的工作实绩践行"两个维护"；注重以"联"促"全"，强化党建与业务的联动评价，对组织绩效"党的全面领导"类指标得分排名后 10%或"税收改革发展""工作运转保障""各方多维评价"类指标综合得分排名后 10%的被考评单位不得评为"第 1 段"，并将组织绩效考评结果向个人绩效考评延伸承接，促进各级税务机关和广大税务干部旗帜鲜明讲政治、沉下心来抓落实；注重以"石"试"金"，针对贯彻落实党中央、国务院重大政策和重大改革任务，制定专项绩效考评办法，把"关键时"和"重大事"作为评价政治素质的"试金石"，既看日常工作中的担当，又看大事要事难事中的表现，从担当作为中考出对党忠诚的精神状态和作风状况。二是破解"多头重复考、统筹不到位"的难题。税务总局在实施绩效管理之初全面清理原有考评项目，该整合的整合，该精简的精简，该纳入绩效考评的纳入，该归入日常工作的归入，并将税务系统考评与地方党政考评统筹起来，实现绩效管理"一张网、全覆盖"，防止"政出多门"，并严禁单纯为考评而要求基层填表报数、撰写报告，严禁能从信息系统中取数仍要求基层报送数据报表，严禁绩效指标搞层层加码等，力戒形式主义、"烦琐哲学"，力求精简易行、管用有效。三是破解"定性考评多、定量考评少"的难题。秉持"干什么考什么"的理念，依托金税工程建设，通过完善"信息系统＋业务应用＋内控绩效"的"大三角"架构体系，不断提升机生机汇机考水平，将组织绩效量化机考指标分值权重逐步提升到80%以上。既考"干没干"，对工作进度和完成数量进行考评；更考干得"好不好"，强化年度间重点工作纵向比较，对工作质量和实际成效加强量化考评，让客观数据说话，防止凭主观印象打分。四是破解"重结果考评、轻过程考评"的难题。实行督考合一机制，将绩效目标节点化，采取节点监控，在不同节点相机进行督查督办，推动绩效执行落地见效；在督查督办工作中建立台账，实行月调度、季通报、对账销号，以督促考、以考强督。将实地督查发现问题或未在规定时限办结的督办事项清单推送绩效办，经绩效办复核后反馈相关考评部门，既在年终考评"算总账"，又在年度中间"算细账"，促进及时纠偏、强化过程监控。五是破解"信息渠道窄、数据不全面"的难题。在推动打通内部各方数据归集路径的同时，不断拓宽采集外部考评数据的渠道，综合运用中央巡视、国务院大督查、外部审计、内部巡视巡察以及政府公共网络信息平台、各类检查评比结果和通报文件，推送相关考评司局实施考评；既将地方党委政府对当地税务部门的考评结果纳入税务系统考评，又将税务系统的考评结果向当地党委政府反馈，实现税务系统与地方党委政府考评信息互通互用；坚持走群众路线，加强常态化了解，多到现场看，多见具体事，多听群众说，注重第三方评估，更多关注税收改革发展、政策落地情况和纳税人缴费人获得感、满意度。六是破解"偏于看一时、失于看长远"的难题。坚持促进可持续发展，组织绩效统筹前后年度考评，加大"自己跟自己比"的纵向比较，对进步明显的给予加分激励，对连年进步最突出的单位，给予增加干部选拔任用或公务员考核优秀名额的激励。坚持全面、历史、辩证看待干部，注重一贯表现和全部工作，将惩在当前、奖在长远和考在平时、管在长远相结合，通过打通各个考评周期、动态运用考评结果，既防止"想比不好比、对比不科学"，又防止"一考定终身"，在干部选拔任用中连续看三年的绩效成绩，当年绩效成绩落后虽受影响，来年绩效成绩提升又有机会，以促进干部持续进步、不断成长。七是破解"操作不简便、费时又费力"的难题。通过开发运行专门的绩效管理信息系统,让绩效考评走出手工操作费时费力的困境,在被考评者无感的情况下接受考评;干部每周在线记录工作日志,每半年用 5—10 分钟进行一次投票测评,数据自动生成,不增加干部负担;领导干部通过系统平台,既可分配任务、评鉴打分,还可随时查看干部日常工作情况,为进一步加强干部平时管理增设了窗口和手段。八是破解"考评者不硬、被考者不服"的难题。监督"考评者",通过意见反馈、以下评上等方式,将考评者置于被考评者的监督之下;考评"考评者",对总局机关司局考评指标进行评议,不定期对司局的考评职责履行情况采取随机抽查方式进行核查,重点对没有扣分的指标考评情况进行核查,对画像精准、考出差异者给予加分激励,反之予以减分约束;建立被考评者申诉机制,考评委员会对考评不准不公的予以纠正。各级税务机关在统一领导的原则下,落实"分级管理"要求,对本级机关和下一级税务局实施绩效管理,结合自身实际编制指标、实施考评、更好体现地域和部门的差异性,确保绩效考评公开公平公正公认。从税务总局到省局、市局、县局,一级抓一级,压实考评者责任,消除了考评者"抹不开面子""下不了硬手"的思想，对考评的尺度把握得更严了，考评成绩的差距也在不断拉开，并通过开展约谈、分析检查等机制，既确保考评动真碰硬，又促进考评发现问题整改到位。2020 年 3 月，税务总局组织各省税务局领导班子全体成员、全体处长和其他干部代表进行网上无记名测评，结果显示对"指标编制情况"的满意度为 96.31%，对"绩效考评情况"的满意度为 91.97%。

Chapter
六

# 关于"税务绩效管理的积极效应"

近十年来，税务绩效管理围绕贯彻落实习近平总书记重要指示批示精神和党中央决策部署、服务"国之大者"、推进税收现代化，在促进提高税收工作质效、提升纳税人缴费人满意度、提振税务干部精气神中的积极效应不断显现，概括起来就是"四个发挥"。

## （一）围绕坚决做到"两个维护"发挥"主抓手"效应，推动党对税收工作的全面领导

一是推动政治机关建设走深走实。通过将"党的全面领导"作为组织绩效指标体系"四大板块"的"第一板块"，把"学习贯彻习近平新时代中国特色社会主义思想"作为第一指标，设置"政治机关建设"关键绩效指标，将组织

绩效管理与个人绩效管理贯通起来，引导各级领导班子和广大税务干部不断增强政治判断力、政治领悟力、政治执行力，持续推动走好第一方阵，促进发挥党组织战斗堡垒作用和党员先锋模范作用，确保坚定捍卫"两个确立"、坚决做到"两个维护"。二是推动党建引领作用抓牢抓实。通过设置"纵合横通强党建"指标并实行专项考评，并将党委书记、党支部书记党建工作述职评议结果纳入绩效考评，督促各级领导班子把抓好党建作为最大的政绩，完善各项举措，用好"条""块"两种资源，建立健全与地方党委及其工作部门重要情况相互通报、考核结果相互推送等机制，扎实推进税务系统党的建设高质量发展。2021年4月，中央组织部组织二局在税务系统开展专题调研，并以《工作通讯》形式刊发《扛起主体责任 汇聚各方力量 推动税务系统党建工作创新发展——税务总局"纵合横通强党建"工作机制的调研报告》，报告全文在《人民日报》（2022年1月12日）和《中国组织人事报》（2022年1月13日）刊登推介。三是推动全面从严治党压紧压实。通过将贯彻《党委（党组）落实全面从严治党主体责任规定》《关于加强对"一把手"和领导班子监督的意见》，落实《税务系统全面从严治党主体责任和监督责任实施办法》，加强对省局"一把手"监督重点事项清单等纳入绩效考评,促进层层压实全面从严治党主体责任;通过完善"一体化综合监督"指标,将构建一体化综合监督体系、内外部监督检查发现问题及整改情况等纳入考评,深入推进构建一体化综合监督体系,全面压实从严治党监督责任;通过将落实深化税务系统纪检监察体制改革试点"1+7"、一体化综合监督"1+6"制度文件要求纳入考评,并制定《省级税务机关纪检机构及其主要负责同志履职考核办法(试行)》,为深化税务系统纪检监察体制改革提供坚强保障;通过设置"正风肃纪"等指标,将落实中央八项规定及其实施细则精神、信访线索处置、"一案双查"机制及廉政警示教育等纳入考评,同时从违纪违法"有没有"、主动办案"查没查"、执纪问责"严不严"、整体情况"好不好"四个维度综合考评,有力促进一体推进"三不腐"。

## (二)围绕推动高质量发展发挥"指挥棒"效应,推进中央决策部署在税务系统落地落好

一是推进圆满完成组织税费收入目标。通过设置"组织税费收入""社保费和非税收入管理"等指标并加强考评,引导系统上下树牢税费皆重理念,坚持在"平稳、协

调、安全、持续"上下功夫，齐抓共管做好税费收入组织工作，始终把依法依规贯穿于组织收入全过程，严肃组织收入纪律，坚决不收"过头税费"，健全税费收入质量监控和分析机制，利用大数据完善分区县、分税种、分费种的收入实时监控体系。2013 年至 2021 年，全国税务系统在减税力度不断加大、宏观税负逐步下降的基础上，累计组织税收收入 112.1 万亿元，连年圆满完成收入任务，为经济社会发展提供了坚实的财力保障。二是推进实打实、硬碰硬落实好减税降费政策。认真贯彻落实习近平总书记"减税降费政策措施要落地生根，让企业轻装上阵"① 等重要指示批示精神，通过设置"税费优惠政策落实"等指标以及制定"实施减税降费"类指标考评方案、退税减税政策落实工作专项考评办法，促进建立减税降费政策直达快享机制，努力以最快速度、最大力度、最优效率确保政策红利第一时间惠及市场主体，确保减税降费政策精准、全面、细致落实到位。2013 年至 2022 年累计新增减税降费及退税缓税缓费预计达 13 万亿元。三是推进全面依法治税。通过对税收法治建设相关工作加强绩效管理和考评，促进

---

① 《国家主席习近平发表二〇一九年新年贺词》，《人民日报》2019 年 1 月 1 日。

全面落实税收法定原则。现行 18 个税种已有 12 个完成立法。同时，积极推进增值税法、消费税法、土地增值税法等立法工作，构建完备的税法体系取得新进展。四是推进全面深化税收改革。通过对实施增值税改革、完善企业所得税制度、逐步建立综合与分类相结合的个人所得税制、构建"绿色税制"体系等设置关键绩效指标，并对营改增、个人所得税改革、国税地税征管体制改革、落实《关于进一步深化税收征管改革的意见》等重大改革事项实行专项考评，确保打赢了一场接一场的改革攻坚战，促进了税收职能作用有效发挥。五是推进持续优化税收营商环境。通过设置"深化'放管服'改革""优化税收营商环境""纳税人满意度暨税务部门政务服务'好差评'""服务'一带一路'建设""国际交流与合作"等指标并加大绩效考评力度，促进以税务人的"用心"，换来税费服务举措的"创新"和税收营商环境的"清新"。第三方开展的纳税人满意度调查结果显示，综合得分 2014 年为 82.06 分，2016年为 83.61 分，2018 年为 84.82 分，2020 年为 86.1 分，2022 年为 89.18 分，纳税人缴费人满意度持续上升。世界银行发布的《营商环境报告》显示，我国纳税指标排名不断提升。六是推进建立健全税务监管体系。通过设置"税务执法督察""税收风险管理""税务稽查管理"等指标和严格考评,把税收法律法规规章和规范性文件的执行,巡视、督查发现问题整改,充分运用"信用＋风险"动态监管机制,重点税源和行业税收专项规范,"双随机、一公开"监管情况等纳入考评,推进健全完善税务监管体系、加强税收监管和税务稽查。

## (三)围绕抓好"关键少数"带动"绝大多数"发挥"传动轴"效应,激发税务干部队伍干事创业动力活力

一是激发各级税务局班子主动谋事抓事。通过将全面贯彻《2019—2023 年全国党政领导班子建设规划纲要》等纳入绩效考评,实行"一把手"个人绩效与组织绩效全面挂钩、班子成员个人绩效与组织绩效按一定比例挂钩,深化绩效考评结果运用,推动既按照优化年龄结构、改善专业结构、统筹气质特征等要求选优配强各级领导班子,又采取切实措施不断提升班子成员特别是"一把手"政治素质和履职本领,当好税务干部队伍的"领头雁"。中央组织部对税务总局党委开展的干部选任"一报告两评议"满意率每年都有新的提升,2018—2020 年分别为 95.2%、

96.3%、98.8%，36 个省、市、区和计划单列市税务局党委的满意率总体上也不断提升，2021 年度结果显示平均满意率为 99.95%，同比提高 0.38 个百分点，其中 34 个省级局达到 100%。在 2018 年的机构改革中，针对领导干部超配、"正转副"等突出问题，注重发挥绩效考评的"催化剂"和"润滑剂"作用，促进安排"正转副"干部到上级机构或本人原工作地任职、到省内原户籍所在地或子女配偶工作地工作、推荐到地方任职、到党校参加培训等一系列措施的落实，并推动各级税务机关开展多轮涉及 130 余万人次的谈心谈话，做深做细思想政治工作，确保了机构改革任务平稳落地，当年税务系统的信访量不仅没有增加反而较 2017 年下降 20%以上。二是激发广大税务干部积极向上向善。通过搭建起晒业绩、比贡献的绩效管理"赛马场"，用好用活考核考评结果，营造"前有标兵带、后有追兵赶、人人不甘落后、事事都想争先"的"大气候"，无形之间给广大税务干部以鼓励鞭策，形成"奋'绩'争'效'"的氛围。尤其通过编制组织绩效指标和个人绩效指标，不仅帮助和促进干部正确处理岗位职责和全局工作的关系，增强工作的计划性、统筹性、前瞻性，而且促进干部把个人成长发展与税收改革发展有机结合起来，树立

"让吃苦者吃香、有为者有位、出力者出彩"的鲜明导向。为每名干部建立个人成长账户，并与培养、使用、管理挂钩，用大数据定位"差距"，激励干部用日积月累的努力为个人账户"充值"，避免因庸懒懈怠形成人生"负债"，促进干部价值观念、思维模式和行为方式的转变，引导各层级各年龄段干部自我约束、自我加压、自我提升。三是激发税务系统上下同心创先争先。绩效管理使得税务总局抓司局和省局、司局抓自身处室和省局对口业务、省局抓处室和市局、市局抓科室和县局等科学有效贯通起来。每一级党委对上级党委的绩效指标进行科学合理的承接分解，转化为对本级和对下一级的管理要求，同时将本级的情况通过绩效沟通及时向上级反馈，形成上情下达、下情上达的管理闭环，撬动每一级税务局既管好本级机关、又带好下一级税务局，既自上而下决策指挥、又自下而上请示报告。各级税务局党委之间、各位领导和干部之间进行常态化绩效沟通反馈，促进一级对一级负责、一级带动一级，拧紧从税务总局"最初一公里"到基层"最后一公里"乃至到每位干部"最后一公分"抓落实责任链条，确保各项决策部署层层负责落实落地、人人尽责落细落好。绩效管理就像一个作出决策、部署任务的"指挥系统"，一个压实责任、贯彻落实的"驱动系统",一个发现问题、补齐短板的"检测系统",一个奖优罚劣、促人向上的"动力系统",激励税务干部一生向上、一心向善,促进税收事业一片生机、一派生气。

## （四）围绕创新行政管理发挥"探路仪"效应，提供构建政府治理体系的税务经验

一是为深化政府绩效管理研究作出理论贡献。兰州大学管理学院名誉院长、政府绩效管理研究中心主任、教授包国宪通过深入税务系统连续两个多月的调研,认为"税务部门实施绩效管理是'真干''实考'""实现了从管理到治理的飞跃""为学界提供了一个好案例,使理论得到支撑和落地"。中国行政管理学会副秘书长、《中国行政管理》杂志社社长、研究员张定安认为:"税务绩效管理对我国政府绩效管理不仅有突出的实践贡献,而且有创新的理论贡献。"二是为推动政府绩效管理发展创造实践样本。2017 年 8 月,时任国家公务员局副局长张义全到税务总局实地调研时认为:"税务总局推行绩效管理和数字人事的做法,是干部人事管理模式的创新之举,是带动干部转变作风、提升素质能力、激发干事创业热情、打造税务铁

军的强有力抓手，实现了传统人事管理与信息技术的有机
融合，实现了干部管理精细化、科学化，为解决不作为、
慢作为、乱作为问题开出了很好的药方，成效显著，超过
预想，令人为之一振，走在了全国前列，为全国公务员考
核工作提供了一个鲜活的案例和样本。"三是为破解政府
绩效管理难题探索方法路径。原国家行政学院政府绩效评
估中心独立开展第三方评估认为"税务系统开展绩效管理
工作具有高位推进、上下联动、闭环运行、自我更新的特
点，成效显著，在全国处于领先地位，是中央和国家机关
推行绩效管理的成功典范"①。2016年2月，时任国家发改
委人事司副司长范波带队来税务总局调研税务绩效管理，
认为"税务总局推绩效管理的一些理念和制度机制设计，
如强化班子考评，把机关与系统结合起来进行考评，依托
信息系统公开考评过程，尤其是绩效考评结果运用动真格
等，很有借鉴意义"。2017年12月，时任中央编办监督
检查司司长田玉萍在国家行政学院与世界银行联合举办的
"公共治理现代化国际经验及启示"研讨会上指出："税务
系统推行绩效管理成效十分明显，不仅推动了工作落实，

---

① 国家行政学院政府绩效评估中心：《税务系统绩效管理第三方评估报
告》，2016年，第9页。

而且促进了管理方式转变，激发了内在活力。税务系统绩
效管理是对税收工作的全方位考察，而且考评内容不断扩
大，考评工具不断完善，对各地各部门开展绩效管理探
索、提升治理水平、增强服务能力具有重要的借鉴意义。"
四是为促进绩效管理国际交流提供互鉴经验。2018 年 10
月，世界银行首次发布题为《通过创新和机构协调提升公
共部门绩效》的全球公共部门绩效报告，积极评价中国税
务部门在机构层级多、干部队伍庞大的税务系统成功推行
绩效管理，促进了营改增等一系列重大改革平稳落地，提
升了行政管理效率，优化了税收营商环境，并将中国税务
绩效管理作为"公务员管理"的典型案例向全球推介。①
国际货币基金组织税收管理专家安妮特·岢认为："中国
国家税务总局在全国范围内的绩效管理设计理念与诸多国
际惯例不谋而合，其中蕴含着发达国家税务绩效管理体系
中的大部分特质，比如使用平衡计分卡、运用信息系统的
自动化流程生成考评结果，以及从信息系统中自动抓取可
靠的数据。中国税务绩效管理体系设计得很好，巧妙地将
国家税务总局的战略方向和组织目标有机结合起来。中国

---

① 世界银行：《通过创新和机构协调提升公共部门绩效》，世界银行中国
代表处印，第 76—80 页。

税务绩效管理有助于国家税务总局在优化纳税服务、降低纳税成本，以及推进税收现代化等方面的目标达成。中国税务绩效管理已经取得了长足的发展，尤其是对于中国税务系统这么庞大的组织而言，取得这样的成绩是令人叹为观止的。"①

---

① 《中国税务》编辑部：《外国专家看税务绩效管理》，《中国税务》2019
  年第 12 期。

Chapter 七

# 关于"税务绩效管理的
# 主要启示和展望"

政府绩效管理是深化行政管理体制改革、构建政府治理体系的重要举措。理论界和实务界的专家学者认为，党的十八大以来，税务系统始终牢记税收在推进国家治理体系和治理能力现代化中的责任使命，认真落实党中央、国务院各项决策部署，探索出一条如何更好履职、推进税收治理体系和治理能力现代化的管理新模式。①

## （一）主要启示

税务绩效管理创新为行政管理体制改革积累了经验、

---

① 李亚飞：《税务绩效管理：触及治理灵魂的自我革命》，《瞭望》2020年第 46 期。

提供了实践样本，并折射出政府绩效管理的演进逻辑，从中可以得出"十条管理启示"。

1. 绩效管理是"着眼长远"的战略管理

认真贯彻习近平总书记"要善于进行战略思维，善于从战略上看问题、想问题"①的重要指示精神，具体体现为绩效管理要"有指导、有指挥、有指标"。坚持以习近平新时代中国特色社会主义思想为指导，以构建促进政令畅通、保持上下战略一致性的决策指挥系统为出发点，以发挥绩效指标的"指挥棒"作用为着力点，税务总局党委统筹谋划，强力推动，促进税务系统各级各部门和每名税务干部把握战略全局，融入工作整体，认真履职尽责，做好本职工作，为实现税收现代化战略目标而奋斗。

2. 绩效管理是"全面系统"的整体管理

认真贯彻习近平总书记"构建从中央到地方各级机构政令统一、运行顺畅、充满活力的工作体系"②的重要指示精神，具体体现为绩效管理要"聚纵向、聚横向、聚同向"。坚持围绕中心、服务大局、统筹高效，系统上下层

① 《习近平谈治国理政》第四卷，外文出版社 2022 年版，第 31 页。
② 习近平：《论坚持全面深化改革》，中央文献出版社 2018 年版，第 433 页。

级之间、横向部门之间以及系统"条线考评"与地方党政"块上考评"之间，注重关联性和耦合性，促进纵向联通、横向打通、同向贯通，突出各方共治的综合效益，服务国家治理体系和治理能力现代化。

3.绩效管理是"和衷共济"的协同管理

认真贯彻习近平总书记"把赢得民心民意、汇聚民智民力作为重要着力点"①的重要指示精神，具体体现为绩效管理要"合众意、合众智、合众力"。从绩效管理运行涉及全员、涉及每项业务、每一环节、每个岗位的实际出发，坚持"一切为了群众、一切依靠群众，从群众中来、到群众中去"，突出"绩效管理要走群众路线，人人向上共树税务形象"，通过深入调研、广泛动员，问计问需于基层干部群众和管理服务对象，促进基层和机关互动、管理和服务并重，画好向上向善最大同心圆。

4.绩效管理是"追求卓越"的争优管理

认真贯彻习近平总书记"推进理念思路创新、方式手段创新、基层工作创新，创造性开展工作"②的重要指示

_____

① 《习近平谈治国理政》第三卷，外文出版社 2020 年版，第 95 页。
② 习近平：《论坚持党对一切工作的领导》，中央文献出版社 2019 年版，第 318 页。

精神，具体体现为绩效管理要"重创业、重创新、重创造"。坚持"惟改革者进，惟创新者强，惟改革创新者胜"，围绕绩效战略目标，不断拓展视野范围，拓宽工作思路，发扬创业精神，突出改革创新，注重创造性开展工作，把顶层设计与基层落实结合起来，有破有立、破立结合，既结合实际、自主创新，又兼收并蓄、推动引进消化吸收再创新，持续在更深层次、更高水平、更新境界推进绩效管理不断上台阶。

5. 绩效管理是"克难奋进"的攻坚管理

认真贯彻习近平总书记"改革争在朝夕，落实难在方寸。越是任务重、困难大，越要知难而进、迎难而上"①的重要指示精神，具体体现为绩效管理要"攻难关、攻难题、攻难点"。坚持发扬事不避难、义不逃责、攻坚克难的斗争精神，"从最坏处着想，向最好处努力"，充分估计面临的困难，下定"只要方向正确、意义重大，就大胆试、大胆闯"的决心，以"红军不怕远征难"的英雄气概，知难而进、迎难而上，攻打一个又一个难关、攻破一个又一个难题、攻克一个又一个难点，不断获得新进展、取得新成效。

---

① 《习近平谈治国理政》第三卷，外文出版社 2020 年版，第 127 页。

6. 绩效管理是"递进发展"的升级管理

认真贯彻习近平总书记"以咬定青山不放松的执着奋力实现既定目标"①"制度更加成熟定型是一个动态过程"②的重要指示精神，具体体现为绩效管理要"能推进、能改进、能恒进"。坚持"坚定不移地推、坚定不移地改、坚定不移地用"，采取"先试点、再推开"的稳中求进策略，强化"以绩效管理思维推进绩效管理工作"的持续改进理念，既始终保持随着实践发展而与时俱进的深入推进态势，又能以自我革命的精神对存在的问题进行优化完善，做到不是一事、一时改，而是事事关联改、持之以恒改，实现平稳接续、平滑升级。

7. 绩效管理是"激励约束"的奖惩管理

认真贯彻习近平总书记"坚持严管和厚爱结合、激励和约束并重"③的重要指示精神，具体体现为绩效管理要"抓高线、抓底线、抓长线"。坚持党管干部、激励和约束并重，顶住压力把考核评价结果与干部选拔任用、公务员

①　习近平：《以史为鉴、开创未来　埋头苦干、勇毅前行》，《求是》2022年第1期。
②　《习近平谈治国理政》第三卷，外文出版社2020年版，第127页。
③　习近平：《论坚持党对一切工作的领导》，中央文献出版社2019年版，第199页。

年度考核、评先评优、人才培养等工作挂钩，强化正向激励和负向约束，树立"追求高线有激励、触碰底线有惩戒、长线发展有引领"的绩效导向，确保通过动真碰硬、赓续发力的绩效管理促进干部队伍崇尚实干、永葆活力。

8. 绩效管理是"科技赋能"的数智管理

认真贯彻习近平总书记"把数字技术广泛应用于政府管理服务，推动政府数字化、智能化运行"[①]的重要指示精神，具体体现为绩效管理要"可机生、可机汇、可机考"。坚持"科学技术是第一生产力"，充分运用现代信息技术，既通过绩效管理促进提高信息化水平，又通过信息化建设为绩效管理提供支撑，促进绩效管理更加高效便捷、绩效考评更加客观公正，特别是要适应大数据时代，强化数字绩效理念，以高水准的信息集成提升量化机考水平，以数字化改造、智能化升级为绩效管理赋予新动能。

9. 绩效管理是"内化于心"的文化管理

认真贯彻习近平总书记"文化自信，是更基础、更广泛、更深厚的自信，是更基本、更深沉、更持久的力

---

① 《加强数字政府建设 推进省以下财政体制改革》，《人民日报》2022 年 4 月 20 日。

量"① 的重要指示精神，具体体现为绩效管理要"显人文、显人心、显人气"。坚持培育既具有部门特色又洋溢时代气息的绩效文化，按照"紧扣关键节点、渐次有序推进、逐步全面铺开"的思路，采取全方位、多层次、长流水、呈递进的策略，既在关键节点有声有势，又在日常之中润物无声，凝聚人心、厚植人气，着力提升各级各部门主动抓绩效的思想境界和行动自觉，为实施绩效管理提供深厚文化支撑。

10.绩效管理是"明理增信"的认知管理

认真贯彻习近平总书记"理论来源于实践，又用来指导实践"②"深刻领悟马克思主义及其中国化创新理论的真理性，增强自觉贯彻落实党的创新理论的坚定性"③ 的重要指示精神，具体体现为绩效管理要"明道理、明原理、明机理"。领会好、把握好习近平新时代中国特色社会主义思想的世界观和方法论，坚持好、运用好贯穿其中的立场观点方法，指导绩效管理实践。强化理论思维，做到知

---

① 《习近平谈治国理政》第三卷，外文出版社 2020 年版，第 349 页。

② 习近平：《在经济社会领域专家座谈会上的讲话》，《人民日报》2020 年 8 月 25 日。

③ 习近平：《坚持用马克思主义及其中国化创新理论武装全党》，《求是》2021 年第 22 期。

行合一，坚持"学用研一体化"、实践推进一步、理论研究深入一层。不断增强信心，广泛凝聚共识，遇到管理难题能够找到破解之策，在理论和实践的结合中推动绩效管理向纵深发展。

## （二）未来展望

绩效管理没有最优，只有更优。税务绩效管理实施近十年来，以永远在路上的执着追求更优和更加成熟定型，取得来之不易的成绩，但同时在理论的创新性、指标的科学性、考评的全面性、技术的成熟性、文化的深入性等方面仍存在不足之处，需要再接再厉继续提升。党的二十大对未来 5 年乃至到 2035 年党和国家事业发展的目标任务和大政方针作出了全面部署，新征程赋予了税收现代化新使命。深入学习贯彻党的二十大精神，围绕全面建设社会主义现代化国家，坚定不移推进税务绩效管理，确保充分发挥税收职能作用，以税收现代化服务中国式现代化，需要从"五个进一步"上持续发力。

1.深化绩效管理理论探索：进一步彰显中国化时代化的要求

党的二十大报告指出，中国共产党为什么能，中国特色社会主义为什么好，归根到底是马克思主义行，是中国化时代化的马克思主义行。拥有马克思主义科学理论指导是我们党坚定信仰信念、把握历史主动的根本所在。习近平新时代中国特色社会主义思想是当代中国马克思主义、二十一世纪马克思主义，是中华文化和中国精神的时代精华，实现了马克思主义中国化时代化新的飞跃。新时代新征程对政府治理提出新课题新要求，只有坚持解放思想、实事求是、与时俱进、求真务实，才能深刻把握绩效管理发展的逻辑必然、历史必然和现实必然。面向未来，纵深推进税务绩效管理实践，必须一以贯之加强马克思主义中国化时代化的科学理论武装。坚持以习近平新时代中国特色社会主义思想为指导，坚持好、运用好贯穿其中的立场、观点和方法，立足中国、借鉴国外、挖掘历史、把握当代，从历史和现实相贯通、国际和国内相关联、理论和实际相结合的宽广视角，进一步强化把党的全面领导贯穿始终以凸显政治引领，由群众评判工作得失、检验工作成效以凸显人民至上，紧密结合国情税情推行中国特色绩效管理模式以凸显自信自立，在坚持和继承的基础上持续不断完善绩效管理体系以凸显守正创新，始终聚焦实践面临的新问题想方设法取得新突破以凸显问题导向，通盘考虑组织绩效与个人绩效考评以凸显系统观念，站在政府绩效管理前沿贡献税务智慧以凸显服务大局，进而为加快构建政府绩效管理体系，推动构建具有中国特色、中国风格、中国气派的政府绩效管理学科体系、学术体系、话语体系作出新贡献。

2. 强化绩效管理基本功能：进一步贯彻新时代党的组织路线

党的二十大报告强调，严密的组织体系是党的优势所在、力量所在。各级党组织要履行党章赋予的各项职责，把党的路线方针政策和党中央决策部署贯彻落实好，必须重视和加强干部队伍建设，这是我们党的优良传统和基本经验。围绕建强党的执政骨干队伍，习近平总书记开创性提出新时代党的组织路线，要求一体推进素质培养、知事识人、选拔任用、从严管理、正向激励"五大体系"建设。面向未来，纵深推进税务绩效管理实践，必须一以贯之认真贯彻新时代党的组织路线。从深刻领悟"两个确立"的决定性意义，增强"四个意识"、坚定"四个自信"、做到"两个维护"的高度制定本部门本领域战略目标，注重前瞻性思考、全局性谋划、整体性推进，不断提高政治站位和战略思维，致力于建设一支政治过硬、适应新时代要求、具备领导和推进税收现代化建设能力的税务干部队伍，确保拥有团结奋斗的强大政治凝聚力、发展自信心，在推进税收现代化服务中国式现代化的进程中，更充分发挥绩效管理的指挥棒、风向标、助推器作用，推动统一意志、统一行动、步调一致向前进，激励引导各级税务机关和广大税务干部以更好的状态、更实的作风贯彻落实好中央决策部署。

3. 拓展绩效管理实践成效：进一步推动税收工作高质量发展

党的二十大报告强调，高质量发展是全面建设社会主义现代化的首要任务，必须完整、准确、全面贯彻新发展理念，并对优化税制结构、加大税收调节力度、完善个人所得税制度、完善支持绿色发展的财税政策等提出系列要求，赋予税务部门担当使命、履行职责的更高标准和要求，以高质量绩效管理服务高质量推进税收现代化是题中应有之义。面向未来，纵深推进税务绩效管理实践，必须一以贯之充分发挥税收在国家治理中的基础性、支柱性、保障性作用。进一步提升绩效管理抓班子、带队伍、促落实、提质效的效能，围绕以税收现代化服务中国式现代化的战略目标，科学编制具有引领性、综合性、关键性的绩效考评指标，聚焦充分发挥和拓展提升税收职能作用打造更加严密的绩效管理闭环，突出责任落实，确保权责一致，组织绩效与个人绩效协同一致，推进税收工作提质增效、税收事业更高质量发展、税务部门的行政效率和公信力显著提升。

4.加快绩效管理技术升级：进一步提升数字化、智能化水平

党的二十大报告要求，坚持创新在我国现代化建设全局中的核心地位。大数据时代，数据无处不在，谁拥有数据资源、用活数据资源，谁就拥有未来。大数据是国家治理体系和治理能力现代化的战略资源，推进数字政府建设是构建现代政府治理体系的重要举措，政府对信息的治理，很大程度上是对数据的分析、利用与治理。面向未来，纵深推进税务绩效管理实践，必须一以贯之提升数字化、智能化水平。充分运用互联网、大数据、人工智能等技术手段，积极推动业务与管理一体实现数字化、智能化，不断强化绩效执行数据的机生能力、绩效运转数据的机汇能力、绩效结果数据的机考能力，统筹任务分配、业务流程、岗责体系、信息系统，将绩效考评功能嵌入其中，提升自动化考评水平，提高绩效管理质效。

5.增进绩效管理价值认同：进一步厚植内生性、持久性动力

党的二十大报告提出，推进文化自信自强，铸就社会主义文化新辉煌。文化是一个国家、一个民族的灵魂。文化兴则国运兴，文化强则民族强。任何管理方式，只有将制度的"硬措施"升华为文化的"软实力"，才能更加深入持久地发挥作用。进一步培育内化于心、外化于行、知行合一的绩效文化，是促进各级税务机关和广大税务干部对绩效管理不断从深化认识到提高认知、再到凝聚认同的必由之路。面向未来，纵深推进税务绩效管理实践，必须一以贯之以人为本、以文化人、浇灌培育绩效文化。进一步以社会主义核心价值观为引领，围绕大力弘扬中国精神、传播中国价值、凝聚中国力量，推动形成适应新时代要求的思想观念、精神面貌、文明风尚、行为规范，在绩效管理理念、方式、措施、手段等方面注入固本培元的精神基因，凸显尊重人、关心人、为了人、依靠人、引领人，抓好绩效提升，讲好绩效故事，不断焕发凝聚人心、汇聚共识、集聚动能的聚力铸魂新气象。

英文部分

*English Section*

Since the 18<sup>th</sup> National Congress of the Communist Party of China (hereinafter referred as "CPC"), the Party Committee of the State Taxation Administration (hereinafter referred as "STA") has been deeply studying and implementing General Secretary Xi Jinping's important instructions on "improving the mechanism for assessing the performance of officials" and "putting your heart into implementation", and following the Party's organizational line in the new era and the requirements of the CPC Central Committee for "strictly carrying out performance management". Focusing on the overall goal of achieving tax modernization in the new era with enhanced Party building, improved tax administration and collection and high-quality workforce, the STA promotes a comprehensive performance management system which ensures that duties and tasks are broken down and assigned to individuals in the tax system nationwide to promote implementation and

improve effectiveness, contributing to realization of tax modernization.

General Secretary Xi Jinping pointed out that "to uphold
and develop socialism with Chinese characteristics, we need
to constantly make exploration in practice and theory, and use
the developing theory to guide the developing practice." In the
process of carrying out performance management, the Party
Committee of the STA not only places emphasis upon practice
innovation to promote theoretical innovation, but also attaches
importance to theoretical development to guide the practice,
which have attracted great attention from academia and practical circle. In May 2019, the National Office for Philosophy
and Social Sciences of the Central Publicity Department identified the research project on "Performance Management for
High-quality Development in STA: Practical Development
and Theoretical Research" as a major entrusted project of
the National Social Science Foundation. Tax authorities are
entrusted with a great responsibility for the modernization of
China's system and capacity for governance, especially the
development of the discipline, academic and discourse system

of performance management in government.

Mr.Wang Jun, the leader of the Party Committee of the STA and the project, attached great importance to the research project and composing this book, and mobilized support both inside and outside the tax system. Highlighting the practicality, application and demonstration of performance management, the project report reflected the development of tax cause in the new era. In addition to the origin, significance, current situation, content and methods of performance management, the final report has in-depth and systematic elaboration of the practical and theoretical innovation of tax performance management in the recent 10 years following the basic logic of "Why to do?" "What to do?" "How to do?" "How to guarantee its promotion?" "What's the key to make breakthrough?" "What's the achievements?" and "What are the inspirations and prospects it has taken to us?" The main content of the report includes "4 Aspects" of background, design ideas, "5 steps" of operations, "4 aspects" of support and guarantee, "3 aspects" of key breakthroughs, "4 aspects" of positive effects, "10 aspects" of inspirations and "5 aspects" of prospects.

*Chapter*

**1**

# Background of Carrying out Tax Performance Management

Since the 18th National Congress of the CPC, the Party Committee of the STA has continuously promoted and deepened performance management with an aim to adapt to the general trend of deepening reform in an all-round way, serve the overall development of economy and society and lead the workforce well. In other words, performance management is carried out with requirements from the CPC Central Committee, needs of tax administration and collection, advantages of the STA and reference of practice.

## 1.1 Carrying out tax performance management is the action to practice "Two Upholds" [①]

The Party Committee of the STA keeps in mind General Secretary Xi Jinping's earnest entrustment to lead the tax officials well, earnestly implements the Party's organizational line in the new era and the requirements of the CPC Central Committee on improving the system for assessing the performance of officials and strictly carrying out performance management, and explores and carries out tax performance management to ensure that all tax authorities throughout the country obey the Party's command, take on their responsibilities and spare no efforts to work hard.

---

[①] "Two Upholds" refers to upholding General Secretary Xi Jinping's core position on the CPC Central Committee and in the Party as a whole, and upholding the Central Committee's authority and its centralized, unified leadership.

## 1.2 Carrying out tax performance management is the important starting point to promote tax reform and development

Focusing on the glorious and arduous mission entrusted to the tax authorities in the new era, the Party Committee of the STA explores and carries out performance management. Through enhancing the Party's overall leadership over taxation, putting the function of taxation into full play and building a strong tax workforce, General Secretary Xi Jinping's important instructions on taxation and the major deployment on tax reform and development of the CPC Central Committee could be well implemented.

## 1.3 Carrying out tax performance management is the scientific choice that aligns with the strengths of the tax system

Through in-depth investigation, repeated demonstration, collective decision-making and extensive mobilization, the Party Committee of the STA fully leverages the organizational, business, standardized management and information technology advantages of the tax system, which is reflected by vertical administration along tax authorities from the STA headquarter to the provincial, municipal, county-level and countryside-level tax authorities, parallel business requirements in Party building, tax administration and collection and tax official management, standardized system and rules in continuously enhancing Party building, tax and fee service, tax administration and collection and inner controlling, and improved Golden Tax Project adaptive to the digital era. The STA explores and carries out performance management in accordance with the actual situation of the tax system and promotes the development of tax cause in tune with the times.

## 1.4 Carrying out tax performance management is the innovation based on the practical experience of relevant parties

The Party Committee of the STA keeps broadening its vision, and drawing lessons extensively from the early practice of relevant departments and local governments, as well as the traditional culture of performance evaluation in ancient China and the practices of foreign governments and their tax departments, and explores and carries out tax performance management. In view of the problems faced by some other departments in performance management, it seeks breakthroughs through innovation and change.

# Chapter 2

# Design Ideas of Tax Performance Management

Government performance management is an important measure to advance the modernization of China's system and capacity for governance. Following the guidance of Xi Jinping Thought on Socialism with Chinese Characteristics for a New Era and General Secretary Xi Jinping's instructions on taxation, "improving the system for assessing the performance of officials" and "strictly carrying out performance management", the Party Committee of the STA devotes to develop a typical, pragmatic and innovative performance management system characterized by the actual situation of taxation. The design ideas can be summarized as identifying "one strategic orientation", establishing "two wheel-driving system"[①], adhering to "three implementation principles", applying "four basic theories" and highlighting "five inner mechanisms".

## 2.1 Establishing "one strategic orientation"

Based on a profound understanding of General Secretary Xi Jinping's important instructions on "Strategy is to make judgments and decisions from the overall situation, a long-term perspective and the general trend"[②], the Party Committee of the STA focuses on the strategic goal of tax modernization in the new era, and carries out performance management to promote tax authorities at all levels to forge ahead together. First, developing strategy with focus on enhancing political stance and leveraging the advantages. The STA draws a blueprint for tax modernization, which is consisted of enhancing political stance, law-based governance, deepening reform and

_____

① "Two wheel-driving system" refers to the system leveraging the strengths of organizational performance management and digital personnel management.

② Xi Jinping, *The Governance of China Ⅳ*, Foreign Language Press (Version 2022), p. 31.

leading the workforce well, and develops a road map and task book accordingly. Second, improving the strategy through analyzing and bolstering weak points. Insisting on goal orientation and problem orientation, the STA summarizes achievements based on the facts, analyzes the weak points with their own initiative, and keeps updating the strategy of tax modernization and improving the performance management system accordingly. Third, implementing the strategy through taking a progressive approach and making new achievements. Through formulating performance indicator, the STA not only carries out regular management in a certain area, but also pays special attention to the long-term effect from an overall perspective, where strategies are turned into actions and new chapter of tax modernization could be created continuously.

## 2.2 Establishing "two wheel-driving system"

In accordance with the *Regulations on the Assessment of Leading Cadres* issued by the General Office of the CPC Central Committee, and the requirements of the Organization Department of the CPC Central Committee on improving the system of performance assessing for high-quality development and carrying out pilot program of civil servant performance management, tax performance management consists of organizational performance evaluation, which focuses on assessing the performance of the leading group, and individual performance evaluation, which focuses on assessing the performance of tax officials. First, establishing a "4+4+4+N" organizational performance management framework. There are 4 major categories of evaluation objects: departments in the STA headquarter, provincial-level tax authorities, special commissioner's offices and deputy provincial-level municipal tax authorities. There are 4 major categories of performance indicators: Party's overall leadership, tax reform and development, operation safeguards and multi-dimensional evaluation of all parties. There are 4 major sources of performance indicators: annual work plan at the beginning of the year, requirements of the "Two Sessions"[1], new tasks in the middle of the

────────────

[1]　"Two Sessions" refers to the annual sessions of the National People's Congress (NPC) and the National Committee of the Chinese People's Political Consultative Conference (CPPCC).

year and the others. Besides, the STA carries out "N" (several) special evaluations for hard nuts. Second, establishing a "1+4+1" individual performance management framework. "1" refers to "one strong foundation"-basic professional capacity. "4" refers to "four pillars"-regular evaluation, public recognition, professional competency and leadership. "1" refers to "one roof"-digital evaluation application. In practice, the organizational performance management acts like a "locomotive" to lead the development through strictly managing the leading group, while the individual performance management acts like the car body to promote the development through managing the officials well.

## 2.3 Adhering to "three implementation principles"

Following the basic rules and strategies of promoting reform and innovation, the STA fully understands that performance management is both an advanced management tool and a challenge for all countries, and insists on three principles when carrying out performance management. First, firmly promoting it. In 2014, the STA developed an overall layout for performance management including conducting trial in the first year, producing effects in the second year, earning a reputation in the third year and on this basis continuously making new achievements step by step. Second, firmly improving it. In line with continuous improvement-the core principle of performance management, the STA insisted on solidifying the foundation, leveraging the strength and tackling areas of weaknesses, and kept improving the framework, indicators and rules of performance management in the spirit of self-reform. In the past 10 years, the STA kept upgrading it once a year and have formulated a total of 10 versions of performance management system, through which its mechanism and system became more mature and established. Third, firmly applying the results. With a strong awareness of "applying it or losing it", the STA takes the application of the performance results as the source that keeps the performance management going, and under high pressure applies the results to multiple issues in a fair and reasonable way, such as official promotion, annual appraisal, talent cultivation, awards and honors, etc. In this way, the STA strengthens officials' awareness of performance management, forces performance improvement, and promotes the spirit and system of performance management to take roots in tax authorities.

## 2.4 Applying "four basic theories"

The STA insists that "The value of theory is reflected by practice". It learns from modern management theory and applies it into strategy planning, objectives setting, implementation, process controlling and the coordination between organizational and individual performance management in light with the concrete realities in a creative way. First, the strategic management theory. According to the core idea of the theory that strategic plan should be developed to meet the long-term development direction and promoted with concrete measures, the STA develops its performance management system according to the tax modernization strategy with an overall view, long-term perspectives and thorough solutions, which guides tax authorities and officials at all levels to not only keep their nose to the grindstone but also look to the future. Second, the objective management theory. In accordance with the core idea of the theory that long-term strategy shall be turned into annual plan and indicators should be developed and responsibilities be identified accordingly, the STA emphasizes that each position should take its responsibilities, breaks down annual key tasks and assigns them to the tax authorities, departments and individuals, so as to promote the realization of strategic objectives. Third, the comprehensive quality management theory. According to the core idea of the theory that there should be a whole-process quality control (PDCA cycle) over task implementation, the STA develops a virtuous circle for performance management of "Strategy-Objectives-Execution-Assessment-Awards/Punishment-Improvement", to ensure a high-quality development of taxation. Fourth, the theory of organizational behavior. According to the core idea of the theory that we should study the organizational development from the view of psychology, physiology and sociology, the STA promotes the improvement of individual performance through carrying out ideological and political work in a meticulous and deep-going way and allocates human resources in a scientific and reasonable way. Upholding the people-oriented principle, the STA places importance on cultural-ethical enrichment and mental health, promoting the advancement of both tax officials and organizations.

## 2.5 Highlighting "five inner mechanisms"

The STA carries out in-depth studies on the principles and gateways to leverage the positive function of performance management, and elaborately sets up inter-related rules and mechanisms that reinforce each other. First, giving pressure and requiring tax authorities to taking on their responsibilities. Based on the deployments and requirements of the CPC Central Committee on "strictly carrying out performance management, emphasizing accountability and ensuring a close alignment between the authority and responsibility", the STA establishes a performance management paradigm where duties and tasks are broken down and assigned to individuals throughout the country. In this way, the STA gives pressures to local tax authorities and stimulates the vitality of tax officials, and develops a performance management system that defines clear duties, brings together tax officials' strength and supervises over tasks implementation strictly. Second, developing close interactions and keeping making improvement. To establish a closed-loop management cycle, the STA develops inter-connection between the organizational performance management, which emphasizes on "making annual plans, implementing the plan, evaluating the implementation, giving awards/punishment upon evaluation, and making improvement upon awards/punishment", with the individual performance management, which emphasizes on "managing tax officials in daily operations, conducting daily management through performance indicators, formulating digital indicators, digitalizing the management in an progressive way, making performance results comparable, applying the performance results and enhancing the demonstration effect of the application". In this way, the STA establishes a close-linked, optimized and reinforced performance management system. Third, carrying out multi-dimensional evaluation to make precise assessment. Since management can be considered as an art, and different objectives may have its own advantages and disadvantages if evaluated from different perspectives, the STA introduces the Balanced Scorecard (BSC) into performance management, and decides the evaluators and period, as well as the assessment of quantity, quality, effect in a comprehensive way. In this way, the STA establishes a multi-dimensional, continuous and comprehensively-balanced performance management system. Fourth, giving awards and stimulating vitality to encourage improvement. To mobilize the workforce and strengthen their seif-motivation, the STA deepens the application of the performance results with positive incentives as the main measures, equipping tax authorities and officials with a strong sense of performance management, competition and advancement. In this way, the STA develops a performance management system with incentives, spur, positive and upright culture. Fifth, enhancing communication and interaction among tax authorities and local governments. Based on the fact that local tax authorities all function under the dual leadership of the STA and local Party Committee and governments where the STA plays the mainstay, the STA coordinates the evaluation carried out in the tax system with evaluations by local governments, the evaluation upon STA headquarter departments with the evaluation upon provincial tax authorities, evaluation by taxpayers and fee-payers with evaluation by tax officials, with an aim to build a paradigm of tax co-governance, improve tax compliance and social satisfaction, and establish an open, coordinated and integrated management system.

# Chapter 3

# Operational Process of
# Tax Performance Management

In compliance with the guiding principles of the CPC
Central Committee to improve the mechanism of administrative decision-making, execution, organization and supervision, performance management in the STA is integrated into
the process of administration and promoted with tax decision-
making, execution, organization and supervision in an integrated method. The operation process can be summarized as 5
steps: developing performance indicators scientifically, promoting execution steadily, carrying out performance evaluation
in an orderly manner, deepening the application of the performance result and committing to performance improvement.

## 3.1 Developing performance indicators scientifically

First, determining the development procedure. Performance indicators are developed in the process of "studying and proposing the indicator developing approach- drafting performance indicators- improving the indicators through several rounds of communication- soliciting opinions extensively-publishing after centralized review and approval in a democratic way". Second, formulating the indicators. The STA insists on formulating organizational performance indicators that demonstrate the governance of China, characterize tax administration, reflect strategic objectives and reinforce the key tasks in accordance with the principles of General Secretary Xi Jinping's important instructions, the deployment of the CPC Central Committee and the State Council, and the objectives of serving high-quality development and advancing tax modernization. Meanwhile, the STA attaches importance to the coordination between organizational performance management and individual performance management, and taking political building as the overarching principle, develops an individual performance indicator system that reflects the differences among different positions and the integrity, ability, diligence, performance and incorruptibility of tax officials. Indicators are developed in accordance with their organizational vision, job responsibilities and their own situation, and are conducive to teamwork. Third, developing the evaluation criteria. The STA decides the period, quality and outcome criteria for indicators in accordance with the actual situation of taxation and the Locke's goal setting theory, avoiding setting up too high/low or too complicated/simple criteria and enables them realizable, controllable and measurable at utmost. In this way, tax authorities and officials have a clear understanding about what to do, how to do, to what extent and within what time limit. Fourth, deciding the scores and weight. The full marks of organizational and individual performance management are 1000-level and 100-level respectively, and the score and weight of each indicator is determined by its category, workload, difficulty and certain management requirements. The STA formulates indicators of provincial tax authorities, and tax authorities formulate indicators of their internal departments and tax authorities at lower levels accordingly. A vertical evaluation chain from the STA, to provincial, municipal, county-level and grassroots-level tax authorities is established, and horizontally, the STA, provincial, municipal, county-level and grassroots-level tax authorities also evaluate their internal departments respectively. Furthermore, each tax official formulates its own performance indicators accordingly. As the saying goes, the body employs the arms and the arms employ the fingers without any difficulty, then the country runs as a whole. In this way, performance management reaches an outstanding effect.

## 3.2 Promoting execution steadily

First, breaking down and assigning the indicators to each position and tax official. The STA advances the implementation of key tasks through steadily promoting indicator execution, and emphasizes that everyone shoulders his responsibility. In terms of organizational performance, the responsible departments of simple indicators are determined by their functions, and the leading departments and supporting departments for comprehensive indicators are determined in accordance with the actual situation. In individual performance management, organizational performance indicators are broken down and assigned to tax officials based on the complete post and responsibility system, and thus a successive chain of "organizational performance indicator-performance indicator for departments-individual performance indicator-responsible tax official" is established. In this way, the goals of tax officials all come from and work for the objectives of the organization. Second, enhancing communication and guidance. The STA advances the implementation of key tasks through steadily promoting indicator execution, and emphasizes that communication shall be smooth and guidance shall be provided, so as to equip tax officials with a clear mind, active working attitude and a path for solution. The evaluator should have frequent communication and give frequent guidance to the evaluated throughout the whole process of performance management, including planning, execution, analysis and improvements. With guidance and monitoring from superior tax authorities and communication and mutual learning from peers, tax authorities are able to develop good solutions to task implementation and performance improvement, where communication plays a positive role in lifting bothers and the quality and efficiency of work is improved. As a tax official realized from the practice, "whether in developing indicators or strictly carrying out evaluation, and whether in making analysis or giving awards/punishment, communication is indispensable. Only incorporating communication into the whole process of performance management, can all parties understand each other and reach a consensus." Third, carrying out analysis and comments. The STA advances the implementation of key tasks through tackling the weakness, and attaches importance to making analysis against the benchmark and making comments against the weakness, so as to make the evaluated realize the gap and weakness, promoting improvements and progress in both organizational performance and individual performance. In performance comment, the STA not only points out the reasons and principle, but also set up the benchmark and awards the advanced; and points out the weakness directly, so as to

strengthen the pressure and motivation to making constant improvement. Fourth, conducting process monitoring. The STA
advances the implementation of key tasks through removing
the impediments, and conducts whole-process monitoring and
dynamic follow-up, so as to correct the mistakes in a timely
manner. By collecting related information and data to moni-
tor the execution of indicators in real time, the STA is able
to identify the existing problems, and enhances process and
quality control.

## 3.3 Carrying out performance evaluation in an orderly manner

First, specifying the evaluators. The main bodies that carry out evaluation are the Party Committees of tax authorities
at all levels, and competent leaders and function departments
implement the evaluation. In individual performance management, the evaluators are determined according to the correla-
tion and familiarity among tax officials and the management
relationship. Second, improving the scoring method. Several
scoring methods of indicators, such as direct deduction meth-

od, benchmarking method, ranking method, grading method, quantitative scoring method and distance to frontier method, are determined by different attributes of performance indicators, so as to ensure that the scoring methods, the evaluation and the results are appropriate. Third, strictly following the evaluation procedure. Organizational performance assessment is carried out through a series of steps such as pre-evaluation reminder, reporting by the evaluated, review by the evaluators, review by performance management office, score approval, score publication, feedback on the results, review discussion and dispute resolution. And the individual performance assessment focuses on regular evaluation and is recorded and assessed in a timely manner through weekly records, quarterly evaluation, and annual accumulations of daily work, moral and talent performance. Fourth, strictly enforcing evaluation discipline. Evaluator must not go through the motions, leak the secrets of the evaluation work such as evaluation results, or use the evaluation as an opportunity to seek personal gain. The evaluated must not practice fraud, interfere with or hinder the evaluation.

## 3.4 Deepening the application of the performance result

First, applying to cadre selection and appointment. In order to clearly establish a selection and appointment orientation that emphasizes practical work and achievement, and encourages tax officials to perform their duties and responsibilities in a more vigorous and promising state and strive for first-class performance, the STA deeply implemented the regulations and rules, such as the *Regulations on the Selection and Appointment of Leading Cadres* and *Opinions on Further Encouraging the Cadres to Take on New Roles in the New Era*, and applies the performance results with cadres selection and appointment through increasing or decreasing selection and appointment quotas and setting performance conditions for promotion. From 2015 to 2022, a total of 19 promotion quotas in department or division level with the total quotas have been given to the departments in the STA headquarter whose annual organizational performance results rank the top two or have made the fastest progress in the ranking. Similarly, a total of

14 promotion quotas in department level have been given to provincial tax authorities, and a total of 2 promotion quotas in division level have been given to branches. From 2019 to 2022 , a total of 4689 tax officials in the tax system have been refused to get promoted and considered in cadre selection and appointment for the time being because they rank the last in the individual performance assessment, and the probation period of 344 tax officials have been extended because they rank the last in the annual individual performance management (the last 20% since 2021). In 2020, a department director general was demoted and transferred to other departments because the organizational performance result of his/her department ranked the last for two consecutive years, in accordance with the regulations on the application of performance results. In the selection of deputy department-level cadres in the STA in 2019, two candidates recommended by provincial Party Committee were not approved because their individual performance results were in the second grade for two consecutive years, which did not meet the related regulations of the STA. From 2017 to 2022, the probation period of 1 department-lev-

el and 12 division-level leading cadres have been extended because their individual performance results have ranked the last in the year. In the appraisal of outstanding young tax officials in the tax system in 2020, a deputy director general and 3 division directors in the STA, and 3 deputy department-level cadres were not included in the list of outstanding young cadres because their individual performance results did not meet the requirements. In 2022, a total of 15344 tax officials have been promoted to leadership in the tax system, all of which met the requirements that the annual individual performance results were above the second grade in the past two years and one of them was within the first grade. Second, applying to the annual appraisal. The STA implements the Civil Servant Law and its supporting regulations, and takes the performance result as an important reference for the annual civil servant appraisal through applying the organizational performance result to the "excellent" quota within the limit of civil servant appraisal policy. From 2015 to 2022, a total of 16 "excellent" quotas of civil servant appraisal have been given to internal departments in the STA headquarter whose annual organizational performance results rank the top or have made the fastest progress in the ranking. And similarly, a total of 16 "excellent" quotas have been given to the leading group in provincial tax authorities and 2 "excellent" quotas have been given to branches. Meanwhile, "excellent" quotas are reduced in the departments that have lower ranking in performance results or the ranks fall too much. From 2019 to 2022, a total of 13907 tax officials in 8424 tax authorities have been given additional "excellent" quota in annual civil servant appraisal and 333 tax officials were given "generally competent" or "incompetent" grade. A total of 695 tax officials working in the STA headquarter were given "excellent" grade, whose annual individual performance results were within the first grade. Since 2020, approved by competent civil servant management department in CPC Central Committee, the STA has increased the ratio of "excellent" grade in 26 departments in the STA headquarter, 37 provincial tax authorities and 2 branches based on the annual organizational performance result. Furthermore, the ratios of "excellent" grade in 8094 units in the tax system have been also increased. Third, applying to talent cultivation. Focusing on the strategy on developing a quality workforce of taxation, the STA incorporates the selection, cultivation, appointment and management of tax talents into performance management and formulates *Special Performance Evaluation Measures for the Training of Tax Talents*, developing a coordinated, highly systematic and concerted environment for talent cultivation. Meanwhile, the STA enhances education and training of tax officials on the basis of their individual performance data, and arranges training and practice based on their weaknesses, so as to make up for their abilities. In recent years, 372 Leading Talent trainees have directly participated in the Reform of Tax Collection and Administration Systems of State and Local Tax Administrations, 191 trainees have directly participated in major missions, such as the Individual Income Tax Reform and Reform on the Electronic Invoice, and 2000 trainees have participated in special tasks. They readily take responsibility, ably lead the officials and remarkably keep progress. The talent demonstration effect is significant and they are highly recognized in the STA. At the same time, the STA selects cadres at or above the division level with excellent performance, outstanding comprehensive quality, high foreign language proficiency and great potential for development from the graduated Leading Talent cadres, and sends them to embassies, international organizations or foreign universities for practice or further study for 1-2 years, so as to broaden their international horizons. When they come back, they will be appointed to the tax authorities of the frontier areas of reform and opening-up. These cadres have been fully recognized in their positions. For example, the Secretariat of the Organization for Economic Cooperation and Development (OECD) said that tax officials dispatched by the STA have excellent professional competence and strong dedication. Meanwhile, the STA creates a system of "Learning, Testing, Using and Assessing" to align the learning of tax officials with performance evaluation, which has led tax officials to improve their political theory and tax competency through daily learning and practice. By the end of 2022, there have been more than 60000 strategic talents, leading talents, professional talents and experts in the tax system, twice of that in 2017, which accounted for 8.7% of tax officials in the tax system, and the demonstration effect becomes more obvious. In 2022, there were 440 tax officials selected to provincial tax authorities from grass-roots tax authorities, all of whom met the requirements that the annual individual performance results were above the second grade in the past two years and one of them was within the first grade. Among them, 52% were given priority because their annual individual performance results were all within the first stage in the past 2 years. Fourth, applying to awards and honors. Giving awards and honors to tax authorities and individuals must take performance result as reference. The quota of commencement and awards will be increased for tax authorities with outstanding performance, and the performance results of individuals that get commencement and awards must meet certain conditions. From 2019 to 2022, there have been 20 units commended as advanced group in the national level, and 1608 units commended as advanced group in the provincial level, all of which got "excellent" performance results. There have been 56 individuals commended as advanced individual in the national level, and 1538 individuals commended as advanced individual in the provincial level, all of which got favorable individual performance results. In the STA headquarter, 220 tax officials were commended as outstanding Party member and 40 tax officials were commended as exemplary Party workers, all of which got favorable individual performance results. Fifth, creating more channels for application. The STA takes performance data as an important reference to promote the accountability of leading cadres. From 2019 to 2022, a total of 73 directors of tax authorities or departments have been transferred to other departments because the organizational performance results of their departments ranked the last for two consecutive years. Meanwhile, in accordance with the annual individual performance results and regular individual performance results, a total of 194 tax officials were adjusted to other positions because they didn't take responsibilities or perform their duties. Besides, the STA fully leverages the communication and guidance function of performance management, and constantly enhances the sense of gains, identity and belongings of tax officials through improving ideological and political work and paying attention to compassionate care. From 2019 to 2022, a total of

7.36 million "political birthday" and other holiday greetings have been sent to tax officials, and 383500 tax officials have been awarded honorary certificates of lifelong dedication to taxation. Furthermore, the STA continuously carries out incentives to prevent tax officials becoming couch potatoes. Taking the performance result of the current year and the previous two years into account, the STA increases the proportion of tax officials whose individual performance results are in the first grade for tax authorities that reach "excellent" organizational performance result, and further increases the proportion for tax authorities that get "excellent" organizational performance results for two consecutive years. In this way, the STA guides the departments/officials that have made progress to become better and urges the regressive to catch up, so as to achieve a prospect that everyone reinforces progress. From 2019 to 2022, the proportion of tax officials whose individual performance results were in the first grade have been increased in 40 departments in the STA headquarter, 55 provincial tax authorities and 6 branches in accordance with the organizational performance result in the year (increasing by 5%

for tax authorities that get "excellent" organizational performance result in the year and increasing by 10% for those get "excellent" organizational performance results for two consecutive years, the same below). In 2021, the proportion of tax officials whose individual performance results received the first-grade rating were increased in 12296 departments that got "excellent" performance results in the tax system.

## 3.5 Committing to performance improvement

First, the evaluators give feedback on the evaluation results to the evaluated in a timely manner. In organizational performance management, the evaluators provide feedback on the evaluation results, details and weaknesses on a monthly basis to help making improvement. Also, it publishes the evaluation results to all evaluated departments and tax authorities on a quarterly basis, so as to promote mutual comparison and learning. In individual performance management, the STA sends analysis report to tax officials through information system and the highest score, the average score and the medium score of tax authorities in the same level and same position are

available in the system. Leaders in charge can help tax officials to identify their ranking and clarify the direction of progress and improvements, through making comments on work
or carrying out one-to-one talking. Second, the evaluator and
the evaluated communicate to find out the weaknesses. The
STA develops and improves the mechanism of "Assessment-
Analysis-Improvement-Reassessment" to enable timely analysis on the problems and weaknesses and the reason why losing
the scores. The evaluators are thus able to point out the weaknesses, make suggestions to the evaluated and listen to the
opinions of the evaluated. In this way, the evaluators and the
evaluated communicate and decide the direction, focus and
measures for performance improvement. Third, the evaluated
formulates practical improvement plans timely. Improvement
action plans are generally developed according to the situation
and the person. Meanwhile, the STA coordinates organizational performance with individual performance, and encourages
to take a wider view and to make improvements through daily
tasks, pursuing for "mutual improvement and mutual promotion" in both the organizational and individual performance.

Fourth, the evaluator and the evaluated promote improvement in a joint effort. Through raising ideological awareness, optimizing indicator setting and strengthening execution monitoring, tax authorities at higher and lower levels are able to advance the improvement jointly. In practice, tax authorities take the indicator criteria as the guidance to analyze "how to implement" and "how's the implementation", and incorporate the diagnosed "weakness" into the indicator evaluation in the next stage. Some tax authorities promote continuous improvement through carrying out internal comments, risk investigation, supervision and feedback. Some take insight into the performance result and actively improve the system and mechanism according to the areas that lose scores. Some focus on the key indicators and fully leverage the leading role of key tasks and difficulties. Some further refine the objectives and tasks, clarify the working measures, and constantly improve the quality and effectiveness of the work.

*Chapter* 4

# "Four aspects" of Support and Guarantee for Tax Performance Management

On the basis of the organizational institutional, and technological innovation, the STA is continuously improving the performance management and strengthen its support and guarantee, and striving for support from all parties with a broad vision, which can be summarized as "4 strengthens".

## 4.1 Strengthening organizational leadership

First, the Party Committee holds unified leadership. The Party Committees of tax authorities at all levels strengthen the organizational leadership of performance, with the director

taking overall responsibility and other members of the leading group taking responsibility for divisions in charge through
regularly listening to work reports and studying and deciding
major issues. Second, the performance management leading
group is responsible for the overall management. Tax authorities at all levels establish leading groups of performance management under the unified leadership of the Party Committee,
with the director as the leader of the group, related responsible
leaders as the deputy leader of the group, and directors of
related divisions as members. The leading group of performance management is responsible for the overall deployment
and guidance of performance management, as well as the review and approval of performance management development
plan, regulations and rules, performance plans, performance
indicator, evaluation rules and performance results. Third,
strengthening the coordination of the office of performance
management leading group. The office of the leading group of
organizational performance and individual performance is separately set up in the General Office and the Personnel Department at the headquarter of STA. In provincial and municipal

tax authorities, the office is set up in the evaluation division, while in county-level tax authorities it is set up in the general office to deal with some daily works. Fourth, the evaluation department performs its own functions in performance management. The General Office at the STA headquarter sets up a performance management division specifically responsible for organizational performance management, and the function of individual performance management is specifically undertaken by the civil servant management division of the Personnel Department. After the country's institutional reform in 2018, despite that the overall staffing was reduced, provincial and municipal tax authorities established evaluation divisions specialized in formulating indicators, carrying out performance evaluation, and promoting performance improvement, etc. Fifth, the workforce of performance management takes the initiatives. Tax authorities at all levels have strengthened the workforce specialized in performance management, and built a team of performance management with the specialized cadres as the main force and the liaison officer as the supporting. Sixth, tax authorities, departments and officials at all levels actively participate in performance management. In the chain of performance management, tax authorities and its internal departments are all likely to assume the responsibility of carrying out evaluation and thus become the evaluators, and the same time, they undertake the tasks from the performance indicators, thus become the evaluated. Different positions at all departments and all levels are fully integrated and participate in performance management. Seventh, the performance evaluation committee carries out evaluation democratically. The performance evaluation focuses on whole-process democracy. Under the leadership of the leading group, the performance evaluation committee is responsible for the deliberation and ruling of major issues, including review of evaluation, making analysis and evaluation on the operation of performance management, putting forward suggestions for improvement, deliberating disputes in performance evaluation and responding to complaints from the evaluated.

## 4.2 Strengthening institutional guarantee

First, continuing to improve the institutional system. A

"1+2+4" system of organizational performance management has been developed, which includes "1 guidance"(*the Opinion on Carrying out Performance Management of the STA*), "2 specified measures"(*Measures for Tax Performance Management* and *Measures for the Application of Performance Evaluation Results*), and "4 evaluation rules"(evaluation rules for departments in the STA headquarter, provincial tax authorities, special commissioner's offices and deputy provincial-level cities). A "1+9" system of individual performance management has also been developed, which includes "1 general measure"(*Measures for Carrying out Digital Personnel Management*), and "9 sub-measures"(*Measures for Regular Evaluation on Tax Officials, Rules of Quantitative Scoring in Digital Personnel Management, Guidance for the Formulation of Individual Performance Indicators, Measures for the Orientation Training of New-employed Tax Officials in the Tax system, Measures for External Evaluation Management, Measures for Professional Competency Upgrading, Measures for Leadership Test, Measures for the Application of Performance Results*, and *Guiding Opinion on Deepening*

*the Application of Digitalized Personnel Management Data).*
Second, continuing to enhance institutional identity. In compliance with the unified deployment of the Party Committee
of the STA, tax authorities at all levels, in light of local conditions, guide tax officials to actively recognize and consciously
practice performance management, understand its importance,
and learn its implementation path and solution to the problems, through explaining principles, clarifying regulations,
explaining difficulties and telling good stories of performance
management. In this way, tax officials not only know "how"
but also know "why", and their recognition of performance
management are deepened in the process. Third, continuing
to deepen the implementation of the institutions. With a clear
attitude of "taking a serious action is better than peddling for
one hundred times", the STA require tax officials at all levels
to take the lead in implementation, incorporate the institutions
into tax administration and collection process, and supervise
the execution, so as to maintain the authority of performance
management institutions and promote the compliance. Fourth,
continuing to enhance institutions evaluation. The implemen-

tation of performance management institutions is tracked and evaluated based on its actual situation by lower-level tax authorities and external parts, so as to promote improvement and effective execution.

## 4.3 Strengthening technical support

First, the performance management and the Golden Tax Project promote each other. On one hand, the construction of Golden Tax Project promotes the digitalization of performance management, which enables the traceability of performance data and management process, and improves automatic data generalization and evaluation. On the other hand, the performance management promotes the construction of Golden Tax Project. The STA takes the overall launching and smooth operation of the core system of Golden Tax Project Phase III, the integration and optimization of information system, the establishment of individual taxation management information system and the nationwide-largest cloud platform for government, and the promotion of smart taxation into performance evaluation, so as to ensure their implementation. Second, improving the performance management information system. According to the development of taxation, the STA updates three versions of information system and gradually develops the function of quantitative scoring, automatic data generation, 360° evaluation, multi-dimension analysis report, evaluation result query and digital personnel information sending, so as to fully meet the operational needs of performance management. Third, deepening the interconnection of various systems. The performance management information system is connected to tax administration, decision making and analysis, internal controlling, statistical accounting, Party building, official document, external third-party evaluation and credit reporting system through interface setting, which lays a consolidate foundation for automatic evaluation. Fourth, promote the upgrading of intelligent performance management. All kinds of performance indicators have their source of evaluation data in different information system to varying degrees. To adapt to the digitalization of tax administration and the process of intelligent transformation, the STA gradually realizes automatic evaluation of organizational and individual performance.

## 4.4 Strengthening the use of assistance from relevant parties

The STA listens to the opinions of experts, scholars and colleagues from other departments from the initial stage to the promoting and upgrading stage of the performance management system framework, which advances the whole process of performance management in the STA. First, advancing performance management decision-making. Experts and scholars are invited to participate in the feasibility study and system design of performance management. A symposium attended by experts, scholars, representatives of enterprises and media is held every year to collect valuable suggestions for improving the framework and formulating performance indicators and evaluation rules in a scientific way. Second, advancing the operation of performance management. Experts are invited to be members of performance evaluation committee, and give full play to their advantages of professionalism and objective evaluation to participate in the review and ruling of performance indicator, evaluation result and disputed matters, etc. Third, advancing the training of performance management. Every year, a training course for performance management trainers is held by the STA and experts and scholars of performance management in theory and practice are invited to give lectures, so as to train the backbone of performance management in the STA with joint-efforts. Fourth, advancing the study of performance management. The STA enhances cooperation with relevant experts through establishing joint-research groups, and conducting in-depth research on the mechanism, indicator system, result applications and culture of performance management, which has formed a series of research results and created a strong atmosphere of practice, research, practice again and research again.

*Chapter*
**5**

# Key Breakthroughs in Tax Performance Management

For thoroughly implementing the guiding principle of General Secretary Xi Jinping's important instructions that "fight the tough battles and crack hard nuts, and ensure each undertaking is successful", the Party Committee of the STA has tried every means to find solutions and complete institutions and mechanisms for the long-standing problems, common issues and chronic problems faced by the Party and government departments, especially the tax authorities themselves in strengthening leading group, managing cadres and implementing strict performance evaluation. Therefore, the pertinence, scientificity and effectiveness of tax performance management have been continuously improved.

## 5.1 Trying every means to solve the problems in "rigorous management over the leadership"

Rigorous management over leading groups can lead a good workforce team and promote implementation. It is the primary task of tax performance management to solve the difficult problem on how to rigorously manage leading groups. The first is to solve the problem that the higher level having difficulty managing the lower level. Chinese tax authorities are multi-level, widely-distributed and have long front. Therefore, it is difficult for the higher-level leading group to directly manage the lower-level leading group. According to the strategic objective of continuous improvement of tax modernization, we should clarify the main direction and focus of each year's work, and arouse the spirit of the leading groups of tax authorities at all levels to work together. The second is to solve the problem that the top leader having difficulty managing other members of the leading group at the same level. Members of leading groups get along with each other closely, and the top leader may feel embarrassed to manage the other members. The tax performance management extends from organization to individual, linking the individual performance of the main leader with the performance result of the tax authorities he/she is in charge, and linking the individual performance of the other leading group members with the performance results of their own tax authorities, the departments in their charge and contact tax authorities at the lower level. It promotes the main leader to be the "first responsible person", and promotes the members of the leading group to do a good job in both the departments in their charge and the overall work. The third is to solve the problem that the influence and effectiveness of performance management are inconsistent upon leading groups at different levels. If the motivation and pressure decline progressively during the intermediate process, it is difficult to ensure the implementation of the work deployment from the STA to grass-foot tax service. By distributing the indicators step by step, identifying the responsibilities layer by layer and carrying out the evaluation item by item, the tax performance management not only clarifies the evaluator department of each indicator at the level of the STA,

but also clearly clarifies the responsibility of each indicator

at provincial, municipal and county-level tax service, making

sure nationwide tax authorities could work together to achieve

the implementation of tasks. The fourth is to solve the prob-

lem that only the year-end evaluation for leading groups is

insufficient in the past. The past annual evaluation for leading

groups, which belongs to the ex-post examination, lacks su-

pervision in advance and in the process, and is not conducive

to process control and timely correction. To resolve the prob-

lem above, the performance indicators are determined from

the dimensions of quantity, quality, progress and effectiveness.

The evaluation is carried out on monthly, quarterly, semi-an-

nual and year-end basis. The linkage between supervision and

performance management is established and perfected. Stan-

dards should be set in advance, reminders should be given in

the process, and strict evaluation should be made afterwards,

so as to form the regular mechanism of leading group man-

agement. The fifth is to solve the problem of "loose manage-

ment" with limited award and punishment measures. Due to

the lack of incentive and restraint means to promote the effec-tiveness of leading group management in the past, which leads to the unwillingness to do solid work and strive for the best, the STA links the results of performance appraisal with offi-cial promotion, awards and honors, annual appraisal. The STA combines performance management with the promotion of leading cadres, so as to ensure that the evaluation is practical and outstanding tax officials are rewarded and promoted. The sixth is to solve the problem of "unsustainable management of leading groups" that the subjective initiative is insufficient. In view of the problem of non-sustainable management in the past, we pay attention to persistently cultivating the perfor-mance culture, strengthening the value identity, maintaining excellent conduct, and actively guide the leading groups of tax authorities at all levels to firmly establish correct view of political achievement and enhance the self-consciousness and initiative of taking responsibility. Through managing lead-ing groups effectively, promoting the top leaders at higher level tax service to manage the top leaders at lower tax, the higher leading groups to manage the lower leading groups, the top leader to manage the members of the leading group, and the members of the leading group to take charge of the departments and contacted units more methodically, the tax performance management promotes tax officials to pursue excellence. More and more leading cadres are deeply aware of the significance of performance management. A small number of cadres who had a wait-and-see or even conflicting mentality before have become active participants. They are no longer entangled in whether to conduct performance management, but focus on how to make performance management better, so as to realize the leap from "I am required to do it" to "I want to do it". Some leading cadres think that performance management is "secondary" at the beginning, but they find that it is "important" gradually, and now it has become "necessary"; at the beginning, they regard performance management as extra workload, or even think that it will increase work burden, but now they feel that it is like a habit of work. This is an optimized upgrade from "I work and everyone watches me" to "I work and everyone follows me" and then to "I work and everyone helps me" and "I lead everyone to work".

## 5.2 Trying every means to solve the problems in "rigorous management of staff "

The first is to solve the problem of "inadequate understanding on staffs and their jobs". The individual performance indicators of the tax performance management cover "one foundation and four pillars", which form a cadre evaluation system that values both foundation and development, both outstanding achievements and potential achievements, and strive to accurately "portray" each cadre, so as to improve the accuracy of appraising and identifying cadres. The second is to solve the problem of "not keeping track of performance throughout the year and making a mess of evaluation at the end of the year". The regular assessment results of each cadre are composed of organizational performance-linked scores, individual performance scores, leader's evaluation scores and realistic performance evaluation scores. Especially through the establishment of real-time assessment indicators, the way of "weekly record, quarterly assessment and annual collection" is adopted in the "personal growth account" of cadres, so as to achieve "a daily account, full measurement of work, clear presentation of performance, idleness nowhere to hide", and guide cadres to "be diligent in daily work". The third is to solve the problem of "one-size-fits-all". According to the position level, the personnel are divided into five categories: the principal or deputy of the leading group, the principal or deputy of the department, and other personnel, which are assessed separately. Combining with the requirements of civil servants classified management, the evaluation system of cadres' professional competence is established, which is divided into five categories and eleven levels, such as comprehensive management, tax service, collection management, tax inspection and information technology. The upgrading standards are set step by step, and the grading situation is included in the "Personal Growth Account" to enhance the pertinence of the assessment and avoid the same or similar requirement upon different levels of tax authorities and different contents of tax business. The fourth is to solve the problem of "doing more or less is equal, and doing well or badly is equal". On the basis of quantifying performance indicators, by continuously recording the index data of cadres at all stages of their career, accumulating data from time to time, and accumulating data from year to year, a "holographic image" of the growth trajectory of cadres is formed, so that those who are willing to work, good at work and work well can stand out and be praised and encouraged. Let those who are slow, inactive and chaotic cannot escape notice and be warned and punished, and guide leading cadres at all levels to perform their duties with dedication and devotion to their work. The fifth is to solve the problem of "emphasizing on assessment and evaluation, neglecting improvement and promotion". According to organizational performance tasks, annual key tasks, special tasks and tasks assigned by leaders, individual performance indicators are compiled. Assessment and feedback of results are carried out in a timely manner. More accurate evaluation on tasks is carried out to promote the vast number of tax officials' self-improvement. The sixth is to solve the problem of "overstressing seniority and balance in the matter of selection and appointment". According to the assessment results recorded in the "Personal Growth Account", the results of cadre assessment are ranked comprehensively every year. In the reward and appointment of cadres, priority should be given to cadres who rank at the first level in terms of assessment results. Those staff who rank at the bottom in terms of assessment results for two consecutive years should be adjusted as cadres who are not suitable for their current posts after studied by the Party committee. The accumulation of personal data is not only conducive to the accurate recognition and assignment of these outstanding cadres, but also provides a basis to punish those cadres who are irresponsible, idle and procrastinating. The majority of tax officials feel that performance management has gone through a process from "knowing" to "remembering" and then to "internalizing it", from "acquaintance" to "knowing each other" and then to "staying together". Tax officials are more energetic, more enthusiastic and more motivated in their work.

## 5.3 Trying every means to solve the problems in "strict evaluation"

The first is to solve the problem that "political quality is not easy to evaluate". The STA focuses on strengthening the

Party's overall leadership over tax work, developing organizational performance indicators of political standards and formulating 20-item list of cadres' negative political performance
and any performance related to the list is "one vote veto" item
in daily evaluation and year-end score. In this way, political
standard is the core principle for all levels of tax authorities
and tax officials to fulfill their duties with responsibility. The
STA emphasizes on demonstrating "determination" through
"actions". The STA regards the implementation of General
Secretary Xi Jinping's important instructions, the implementation of the decisions and deployment of the Party Central
Committee, the implementation of new development philosophy, and the actual performance of promoting high-quality development as the basis for setting performance indicators and
carrying out performance evaluation, as well as an important
means for gauging political quality. The STA guides tax authorities at all levels and the vast number of tax officials to
practice the "Two Upholds" in order to promote high-quality
development. The STA emphasizes on promoting "integrity"
through "linkage". To strengthen the linkage between the

evaluations on Party building and tax business, the evaluated units which rank the last 10% of the organizational performance indicators of "Party's overall leadership" or the last 10% of the comprehensive scores of "tax reform and development", "work operation guarantee" and "multi-dimensional evaluation of all parties" can not be rated in the first grade, and the results of organizational performance evaluation are further reflected in the individual performance results. The STA promotes tax authorities at all levels and the vast number of tax officials to take a clear-cut stand on politics and commit to implement it. The STA emphasizes on testing "gold" through "stone". To implement major policies and reform tasks of the Party Central Committee and the State Council, the STA formulates special performance evaluation measures, takes "critical time" and "major events" as the "touchstone" for evaluating political quality. The STA not only evaluates on the responsibility in daily work, but also the performance in major and difficult events, with the loyalty to the Party and the style of work demonstrated through these performance and responsibilities. The second is to solve the problem of "multiple repeated evaluations and inadequate overall planning". At the early stage of performance management, the STA cleaned up the original evaluation items in an all-round way by integrating and streamlining relative evaluation item, incorporating them into the performance evaluation or the daily work, and integrating the tax performance evaluation with the local Party and government performance evaluation. These measures realize "the full coverage through one net" and prevent the problem of overlapping. It is strictly forbidden to require grass-roots tax authorities to fill in forms and write reports simply for performance evaluation or submit data reports when data can be got from the information system. It is strictly forbidden to increase the number of performance indicators by levels, so as to avoid pointless formalism and "redundancy philosophy". Streamlined, simple and effective methods must be adopted. The third is to solve the problem of "more qualitative evaluation and less quantitative evaluation". Adhering to the concept of "evaluating the quality and effectiveness of actual work", relying on the construction of the Golden Tax Project, through improving the "big triangle" system of "information system + business application + internal control performance", we have been continuously improving data-driven evaluation, and gradually increasing the proportion of quantitative indicators in organizational performance to more than 80%. It focuses on not only whether the work is done by evaluating the progress and quantity of the work, but also whether the work is done well by strengthening the year-on comparison of key works between years and the quantitative evaluation on the quality of work and actual results, preventing subjective scoring. The fourth is to solve the problem of "emphasizing on result evaluation and neglecting process evaluation". The STA implements the mechanism which integrates supervision and examination. The STA determines the performance target node, adopts node monitoring, carries out supervision at different nodes, and promotes the effectiveness of performance implementation. The STA establishes journals for supervision and implements monthly schedule and quarterly reporting to urge supervision and improve evaluation. The list of supervisory matters discovered by on-the-spot inspection or not completed within the prescribed time limit will be informed to the performance office, and further informed to the relevant evaluator departments upon the review by the performance office, so as to promote timely correction and strengthen process monitoring. The fifth is to solve the problem of "narrow information channels and incomplete data". While promoting the integrity of internal data sources, we constantly broaden the channels for collecting external evaluation data, and comprehensively use the results of the central disciplinary inspections, the State Council accountability inspections, external audit, internal disciplinary inspection, as well as the government's public network information platform, various inspection and evaluation results and notification documents to help the relevant evaluator departments to implement the evaluation. The evaluation results of local tax authorities by local Party committees and governments are integrated into the evaluation of the tax administration while the evaluation results of the tax administration are transferred to the local Party committee and government, so as to realize the exchange and interoperability of the evaluation information between the tax administration and the local Party committee and government. Adhering to the mass line, the STA strengthens the normalization of investigation by seeing more specific things on the spot and listening more to the masses, lays emphasis on third-party evaluation, and pays more attention to tax reform and development, policy implementation and taxpayers' sense of satisfaction. The sixth is to solve the problem of "having a short-term perspective and ignoring long-term considerations". The STA insists on promoting sustainable development and overall planning of year-on evaluation on organizational performance. We encourage vertical self-comparison. We give extra points to those who have made remarkable progress and give incentives to those that have made the most outstanding progress in successive years by increasing the number of the cadres selected and appointed or the quotas of "excellent civil servants". We adhere to a comprehensive, historical and dialectical view of cadres and pay attention to their overall performance and achievements. We combine punishment at present and reward in the long run with examination in peacetime and management in the long run, and use the evaluation results dynamically through breaking through various evaluation cycles, so as to prevent the problems that "performance comparison is hard and not scientific" and "an exam determines their life". The performance scores of the three consecutive years should be considered when selecting and appointing leading cadres. Although the evaluation is affected by the backwardness of performance in some years, there will be opportunities to improve performance in the coming year, which encourages the continuous progress and growth of cadres. The seventh is to solve the problem of "operation is not easy, time-consuming and laborious". Through developing a special performance management information system, where the performance evaluation can get out of the dilemma of manual operation, which is time-consuming and laborious, and the evaluated accept the evaluation unconsciously. The cadres record their work logs online every week, vote and evaluate once every six months in 5-10 minutes, and the data is automatically generated without increasing the burden of the cadres. Through the information system, leading cadres can not only assign tasks, evaluate and score, but also check the daily work of cadres at any time, thus further strengthening the daily management of cadres in peacetime. The eighth is to solve the problem of "the evaluator is not impartial and the evaluated is not convinced". The STA supervises the "evaluator" by putting the evaluator under the supervision of the evaluated through feedback and retrorse evaluation, and evaluates the "evaluators" through reviewing indicators formulated and carrying out random review on the duty performance of the evaluators from time to time, with a focus on the evaluation of indicators that have no deducted scores. The STA gives incentives to those who are accurate in evaluation and realize differentiated in evaluation results, otherwise constrains those by deducting points; The evaluation committee shall correct the unfair evaluation. Under the principle of unified leadership, tax authorities at all levels implement the requirements of "hierarchical management", implement performance management for tax authorities at the same level and tax service at the lower level, compile indicators and implement evaluation according to their own reality, better reflect regional and departmental differences, and ensure that performance evaluation is open, fair and recognized. From the STA to the provincial, municipal and county level bureaus, the tax authorities at higher level enhance management on the tax authorities at lower level, shoulder responsibilities of the evaluators earnestly, eliminate the idea that the evaluators "fear to offend others" and "manage strictly". The evaluator carries out the assessment more strictly, and the gap between the assessment results is constantly widening. Through the mechanism of interview, analysis and inspection, it not only ensures that the assessment is really strict, but also promotes the rectification of the problems found in the assessment. In March 2020, the STA organized all members of the leading groups in the provincial tax service, all division chiefs and some representatives of other cadres to conduct an anonymous online evaluation. The results showed that the satisfaction rate of "indicator formulation" was 96.31%, and the satisfaction rate of "performance evaluation" was 91.97%.

# Chapter 6

# Positive Effects of Tax Performance Management

Over the past decade, tax performance management has focused on implementing General Secretary Xi Jinping's important instructions and the Party Central Committee's deployment, serving the country's most fundamental interests and promoting the modernization of taxation. The positive effects of tax performance management in promoting the quality and efficiency of tax work, improving the satisfaction of taxpayers and fee payers, and boosting the spirit of tax officials have been constantly emerging, which can be summarized as four aspects.

## 6.1 Focusing on resolutely achieving "Two Upholds", we promote the Party's overall leadership over tax work

First, the STA solidly promotes the construction of political organs. We take "the Party's overall leadership" as the "first part" of "four major parts" in the organizational performance indicator system, take "learning and implementing Xi Jinping Thought on Socialism with Chinese Characteristics for a New Era" as the first indicator, set up the key performance indicator of "political organ construction", and link up organizational performance management with individual performance management. Leading groups and tax officials at all levels are guided to continuously enhance their political judgment, political understandings and political execution, and continue to taking the lead. We promote the role of Party organizations as fighting fortresses and the vanguard and exemplary role of Party members, and ensure that the "Two Establishments" are firmly upheld and the "Two Upholds" are resolutely achieved. Second, the STA firmly strengthens the role of Party building as a driving force. We set up the indicator of "strong Party building in vertical and horizontal dimensions" and carry out special evaluation, and incorporate the review results of Party committee secretaries' and Party branch secretaries' Party building work into the performance evaluation. We urge leading groups at all levels to take Party building as their greatest achievement, improve various measures, and make good use of the two resources of vertical and horizontal management. We establish and improve the mechanism of mutual notification of important information and evaluation results with local Party committees and their working departments, and firmly promote the high-quality development of Party building in tax authorities. In April 2021, the Second Bureau of the Organization Department of the CPC Central Committee carried out a special investigation in tax authorities, and published the report, *Shouldering the Main Responsibility and Gathering All Forces to Promote the Innovative Development of Party Building in the Tax System-the Research Report on the Working Mechanism of " Strong Party Building in Vertical and Horizontal Dimensions" of the STA* on the Work Newsletter. The full text of the report was published in *People's Daily* (January 12, 2022) and *ZHONGGUO ZUZHIRENSHI BAO* (January 13, 2022). Third, the STA exercises full and rigorous governance over the Party, and continues to take responsibility. Through the implementation of *Provisions on the Party Committee (Party Group) Implementing the Main Responsibility of Full and Rigorous Governance over the Party in an All-round Way, Opinions on Strengthening the Supervision of the "Top Leaders" and Leading Groups*, and *Measures for Implementing the Main Responsibility and Supervision Responsibility of Full and Rigorous Governance over the Party in an All-round Way in the Tax system*, the STA formulates a list of key matters of supervision upon the "top leaders" in provincial tax service and includes them into performance evaluation, so as to promote the implementation of the main responsibility of full and rigorous governance over the Party at all levels. By improving the indicator of "integrated comprehensive supervision", we incorporate the construction of an integrated comprehensive supervision system, the problems identified in internal and external supervision and inspection, and their rectification into the evaluation, further promote the construction of an integrated comprehensive supervision system, and comprehensively consolidate the supervision responsibility of full and rigorous governance over the Party. By incorporating the requirements of the institutional documents of "1 + 7" for deepening the reform of the discipline inspection and supervision system in the tax system and "1 + 6" for integrated comprehensive supervision into the evaluation, and formulating *Measures for the Performance Assessment of Discipline Inspection Departments of Provincial Tax Authorities and their Main Responsible Comrades (Trial Implementation)*, performance management provides a strong guarantee for deepening the reform of the discipline inspection and supervision system in the tax system. By setting up such indicators as "integrity and discipline", the implementation of the central Party leadership's "eight-point decision" on improving conduct and its rules for implementation, the handling of public complaints reporting, the mechanism of "one case, two investigations"[①] and the education of incorruptness warning have been included in the evaluation. At the same time, we conduct comprehensive evaluation from four dimensions such as "whether or not" violation of discipline, "whether or not" actively handling of cases, "whether or not" strict accountability for discipline and overall situation, as a result, the tax performance management vigorously promotes the integration of "three non-corruption".

## 6.2 Focusing on the oriented effect of high-quality development, we implement the deployment of the central government in tax system

First, the successful completion of the goal in tax and fee revenue has been achieved. By setting up indicators such

---

① "One case, two investigations" means that investigating tax-related illegal cases of taxpayers withholding agents and other relevant parties, the tax authorities or tax personnel's law-enforcement behavior standardization and duty performance integrity are checked, and the disciplinary and illegal behaviors are investigated and held accountable according to relevant regulations.

as "collecting tax and fee revenue", "social security contributions and non-tax income management" and strengthening
these indicators' evaluation, the STA guides tax authorities at
all levels to firmly establish the concept of both tax and fee
being highly regarded, insist on working hard on "stability,
coordination, safety and sustainability", and achieve the goal
of collecting tax and fee revenue effectively. The tax authorities always run through the whole process of collecting tax
and fee revenue in accordance with the law and regulations,
resolutely refrain from collecting "excessive tax and fees"
and improve the mechanism for monitoring and analyzing
the quality of tax and fee revenue. The STA leverages big
data to improve the real-time monitoring system of revenue
based on different districts and counties or different taxes
and fees. From 2013 to 2021, the tax authorities nationwide
accumulated 112.1 trillion yuan of tax revenue on the basis
of increasing tax reduction and gradual decline in macro tax
burden, successfully completing the revenue task year after
year, and providing a solid financial guarantee for economic
and social development. Second, the implementation of the

policy in tax and fee reduction has been promoted. The STA conscientiously implements General Secretary Xi Jinping's important instructions such as "tax and fee reduction policies and measures should settle down and let enterprises reduce burden". The STA promotes tax and fee reduction policies by setting up indicators such as "implementation of preferential tax and fee policies" and formulates evaluation schemes for "implementation of tax and fee reduction" indicators and special evaluation methods for the implementation of tax rebate and tax reduction policies. Efforts have been made to ensure that policy dividends benefit market entities at the first time with the fastest speed, the greatest strength and the best efficiency, and to ensure that tax and fee reduction policies are implemented accurately, comprehensively and meticulously. From 2013 to 2022, over 13 trillion yuan was added in tax reduction, fee reduction and tax rebate. Third, the STA has promoted tax administration according to law comprehensively. Through strengthening the performance management and evaluation of the work related to the construction of the law in taxation, we promote the full implementation of the principle of legality in taxation. 12 of the current 18 tax categories have been legislated. At the same time, we actively promote the legislation of VAT law, consumption tax law and land VAT law, and make new progress in building a complete tax law system. Fourth, the STA has promoted the comprehensive and deepening tax reform. Through setting up key performance indicators on the implementation of VAT reform, the improvement of enterprise income tax system, the gradual establishment of a comprehensive and classified personal income tax system, and the construction of a "green tax system" and conducting special evaluation on the Reform of Replacing Business Tax with Value-added Tax, the Reform of Personal Income Tax, the Reform of Tax Collection and Administration System of State and Local Tax Administrations, and the implementation of *Opinions on Further Deepening Tax Collection and Administration System*, we have won one battle after another of the reform. It has promoted the effective play of tax functions. Fifth, the STA has promoted the continuous optimization of the tax business environment. By setting up indicators such as "deepening reforms to streamline administration and delegate power, improve regulation, and upgrade services","optimizing the tax business environment", "taxpayer satisfaction and tax service evaluation", "contributions to Belt and Road Initiative" and "international communication and cooperation" and enhancing performance evaluation, we promote the efforts of tax officials in exchange for the innovation of tax service initiatives and the fresh tax business environment. The results of the third-party taxpayer satisfaction survey showed that the comprehensive score was 82.06 in 2014, 83.61 in 2016, 84.82 in 2018, 86.1 in 2020 and 89.18 in 2022, and the satisfaction of taxpayers continued to rise. The World Bank *Doing Business* report shows that China's ranking of tax indicators has been rising constantly. Sixth, the STA has promoted the establishment and improvement of the tax supervision system. By setting up such indicators as "tax law enforcement supervision", "tax risk management", "tax inspection management" and carrying out strict evaluation, we bring the implementation of tax laws, regulations and normative documents, the rectification of the problems found by disciplinary inspection and supervision, the full use of the dynamic supervision mechanism of "credit + risk", the special tax norms for key tax sources and industry and "double random and one announcement"[1] supervision situation into performance evaluation. We have improved the tax supervision system and strengthened tax regulation as well as tax inspection.

## 6.3 Focusing on grasping the "key minority" to activate the "vast majority" and play the leading effect, we stimulate the entrepreneurial vitality of tax staff

The first is to stimulate the leading groups of tax authorities at all levels to take the initiative to work. By incorporating the full implementation of the *Outline of National Party and Government Leading Group Construction Plan for 2019-2023* into the performance evaluation, the individual performance

---

[1]　"Double random and one announcement" means that tax authorities randomly select the inspection objects and the law enforcement inspectors in the supervision process, and timely disclose the inspection situation and the handling results to the public.

of top leaders is fully linked to organizational performance, and the individual performance of leading group members is linked to organizational performance in a certain proportion, so as to achieve fall application of performance evaluation results. The STA promotes the selection of leading groups at all levels in accordance with the requirements of optimizing age structure, improving professional structure and coordinating temperament characteristics. Practical measures have been taken to continuously improve the political quality and the ability to fulfill duty of the members of leading groups, especially the top leaders, so as to be good examples of the tax officials. The satisfaction rate of the "one report and two evaluations"[①] carried out by the Organization Department of the CPC Central Committee has been improved every year, reaching 95.2%, 96.3% and 98.8% respectively from 2018 to 2020. The satisfaction rate of the Party committees of 36 provincial-level tax service has also been improved on the

---

① "One report" means a special report of cadre selection and appointment by the end of year, and "two evaluations" means to evaluate the work of cadre selection and appointment , as well as the selected cadres.

whole. The results of 2021 showed that the average satisfaction rate was 99.95%, an increase of 0.38 percentage points over the previous year, of which 34 provincial tax service reached 100%. In the institutional reform of 2018, in view of the prominent problems such as over-allocation of leading officials and "principal jobs transferred to deputy jobs", we paid attention to the positive function of performance evaluation. The STA conducted a series of measures, such as arranging "principal to deputy" officials to work in the institutions at higher levels or their original working places, to work in their hometown or their children's and spouse's working place, to recommend them to local government posts, and to participate in training in Party schools. We promoted tax authorities at all levels to carry out several rounds of heart-to-heart talks more than 1.3 million times, while did in-depth and detailed ideological and political work to ensure the smooth landing of the task of institutional reform. The number of public complaints reporting to the tax system in that year did not increase, but decreased by more than 20% compared with that of 2017. The second is to stimulate the majority of tax officials to be positive and upward. By setting up a performance management "racetrack" to display performance and compare contributions, we make good use of the evaluation results flexibly, create a "climate" of "pacesetters ahead, pursuers behind, everyone unwilling to lag behind and wants to be the first", which invisibly encourage and spur the vast number of tax officials, and form an atmosphere of "striving for achievements and effectiveness". Especially through the compilation of organizational performance indicators and individual performance indicators, it not only helps and promotes officials to correctly handle the relationship between post responsibilities and overall work, enhance the overall planning and foresight of work, but also promotes tax officials to integrate personal growth with tax reform and development. The STA has established a clear orientation of "rewarding those with more efforts and making contributions". A personal growth account has been established for each official, and linked with training, appointment and management, while the gap among individual performance has been identified by big data, in order to encourage officials to "recharge" their personal accounts with accumulated efforts, avoid the formation of "liabilities" due to idleness, promote the transformation of their values, thinking modes and behavior patterns, and guide tax officials at all ages and at all levels to exercise self-restraint, self-pressure and self-improvement. The third is to stimulate the tax system to work together to take the lead. Performance management enables the STA to focus on its own departments and provincial service, the STA departments to focus on their own divisions and provincial service's counterpart business, provincial service to focus on divisions and municipal service, municipal service to focus on sections and county service. Party committees at each level execute scientific and reasonable acceptance and decomposition of the performance indicators from Party committees at higher levels, transform them into management requirements at the same level and at the next level, and timely feedback to their superiors through performance communication, thus form a closed-loop management from the top to the bottom, and urge each level of tax service to manage their own units and tax service at lower level. It not only makes decisions and commands from top to bottom, but also requests and reports from bottom to top. We conduct regular performance communication and feedback among Party committees, leaders and officials of tax service at all levels, promote the lower level to be responsible for the higher level and the higher level to drive the lower one, tighten the chain of responsibility from the "first kilometer" of the STA to the "last kilometer" at the grass-roots level and even to the "last centimeter" of each official, and ensure that decision-making and deployment are implemented responsibly. Performance management is like a "command system" for making decisions and deploying tasks, a "driving system" for shouldering responsibilities and implementing them, a "detection system" for finding problems and making up for shortcomings, and a "power system" that rewards the good and punishes the bad and aspires people, encouraging tax officials to make progress all their lives and strive for perfection, so as to promote the cause of taxation.

## 6.4 Focusing on the exploring effect of innovative administration, we provide tax experience for national governance system development

The first is to make theoretical contributions to deepening the study of government performance management. Professor Bao Guoxian, honorary dean of the School of Management and director of the Center for Government Performance Management in Lanzhou University, through in-depth research on the tax system for more than two consecutive months, believes that "the implementation of performance management by the tax authorities is a leap from management to governance" and "provides a good example for the academic circles to transform from theory to practice". Zhang Dingan, deputy Secretary-General of China Administration Society, president and researcher of *China Administration Magazine*, believes that "tax performance management has not only made outstanding practical contributions, but also innovative theoretical contributions to government performance management in China." The second is to create practical samples for promoting the development of government performance management. In August 2017, Zhang Yiquan, then deputy director of the State Civil Service Bureau, went to the STA for field research and said, "the implementation of performance management and digital personnel practices by the STA is an innovative move in the mode of official personnel management, and a powerful starting point to drive officials to change their style of work, improve their quality and ability, stimulate their enthusiasm for entrepreneurship and build an iron army of taxation. It has realized the integration of traditional personnel management and information technology, and has realized the refinement and scientificalization of official management. In order to solve the problems of inaction, slow action and disorderly action, it has provided a good prescription, achieved remarkable results, exceeded expectations, inspired people, walked in the forefront of the country, and provided a vivid case and sample for the national civil service assessment work." The third is to explore ways and means to solve the problems of government performance management. The former Government Performance Evaluation Center of the National School of Administration independently conducted a third-party evaluation and considered that "the tax system's performance management work has the characteristics of high-level promotion, up-down linkage, closed-loop operation and self-renewal, and has achieved remarkable results. It is in the leading position in the country and is a successful model for the central and state departments to implement performance management". In February 2016, Fan Bo, then deputy director of the Personnel Department of the National Development and Reform Commission, led a team to the STA to investigate tax performance management, believing that "the STA promotes some concepts and institutional mechanisms of performance management, such as strengthening leading groups evaluation, integrating headquarter departments with nationwide tax authorities for evaluation, relying on information systems to publicize the evaluation process, especially strict application of performance evaluation results. It is of great significance for reference". In December 2017, Tian Yuping, then Director of the Supervision and Inspection Department of State Commission Office of Public Sectors Reform, pointed out at the seminar on "International Experience and Enlightenment of Modernization of Public Governance" jointly organized by the National School of Administration and the World Bank that "the implementation of performance management in the tax system has achieved remarkable results, which not only promotes the implementation of work, but also promotes the transformation of administration methods and stimulates internal vitality. Tax system performance management is a comprehensive investigation of tax work. The evaluation content is constantly expanding, and the evaluation tools are constantly improving, which has important reference significance for various departments to explore performance management, improve governance level and enhance service capacity". The fourth is to provide chances to learn experience mutually for promoting international exchanges in performance management. In October 2018, the World Bank issued its first global public sector performance report entitled *Improving Public Sector Performance through Innovation and Institutional Coordination*, which positively evaluated the successful implementation of performance management by China's tax authorities in the tax system with complex institutional levels and a large number of tax officials, and promoted a series of major reforms such as replacement business tax with value-added tax. The administrative efficiency has been promoted, and tax business environment has been optimized. It also introduced China's tax performance management as a typical case of "civil servant management" to the world. Annette Chooi, an expert on tax management at the International Monetary Fund, said, "The design of the performance management systems in STA across the whole country are very consistent with international practices and contains much of the features we would see in developed countries around the world, like the use of the Balanced Scorecard approach and the linking of the results that are generated in the systems to underlying automated processes and the reliability of the data that is coming from the systems. The systems are designed to very well link in with the goals of the organization and the strategic direction that the STA is trying to move. They support things like the improvements of taxpayer services and reduction in taxpayer costs, as well as supporting the general modernization goals of the STA. The framework is working very systematically. The achievement of implementing such framework is very impressive, almost spectacular achievement to implement it in such a big organization."

*Chapter* 7

# Main Thoughts and Prospects of Tax Performance Management

Government performance management is an important measure to deepen the reform of public administration system and build a government governance system. Experts and scholars from the theoretical and practical circles believe that since the 18th National Congress of the Communist Party of China, the tax system has always kept in mind the responsibility of taxation in promoting the modernization of the national governance system and governance capacity, conscientiously implemented the decision and arrangements of the Party Central Committee and the State Council, and explored a new administration model on how to better perform their duties and promote the modernization of the tax governance system and governance capacity.

## 7.1 Main thoughts

The innovation of tax performance management has accumulated experience and provided practical samples for the reform of public administration system, and reflects the evolution logic of government performance management, from which we can draw ten aspects of inspirations.

### 7.1.1 Performance management is a long-term strategic management

General Secretary Xi Jinping's important guiding principles of "being good at strategic thinking, looking at and thinking about questions strategically" should be earnestly implemented, which is embodied in the fact that performance management should have "guidance, command and indicators". Guided by Xi Jinping Thought on Socialism with Chinese Characteristics for a New Era, starting from the construction of a decision-making and command system that realizes the smooth transmission and implementation of policies and maintains the strategic consistency between the upper and lower levels, and focusing on giving full play to the oriented effect of performance indicators, the Party Committee of the STA has made overall plans and vigorously promoted it. All departments at all levels of the tax system and every tax official grasp the overall strategic situation, integrate into the work as a whole, conscientiously perform their duties and responsibilities, and do their jobs well, striving to achieve the strategic goal of tax modernization.

**7.1.2 Performance management is a comprehensive and systematic management**

The STA should conscientiously implement General Secretary Xi Jinping's important guiding principle of "building a unified government decrees and smooth and dynamic working system from the central to local levels", which is embodied in the fact that performance management should "maintain cohesion vertically, horizontally and in the same direction". Focusing on the central task, serving the overall situation and coordinating efficiency, we should pay attention to the relevance and coupling among the upper and lower levels of the system, among the horizontal departments and among the "line evalu-

ation" of the system and the "block evaluation" of the local

Party and government, promote vertical, horizontal and co-

directional connectivity, highlight the comprehensive benefits

of co-governance of all parties, and serve the modernization

of the national governance system and governance capacity.

### 7.1.3 Performance management is a collaborative management of solidarity

The STA should conscientiously implement General Sec-

retary Xi Jinping's important guiding principle of "winning

the people's hearts and support, gathering the people's wis-

dom and strength", which is embodied in the fact that perfor-

mance management should "unite the people's will, wisdom

and strength". Starting from the reality that the operation of

performance management involves all staff, every business,

every link and every post, we should adhere to the principle

of doing everything for the masses, relying on them in every

task, carrying out the principle of "from the masses, to the

masses", highlight that "performance management should fol-

low the mass line and everyone strives for excellence to build up tax authorities' image", and conduct in-depth research and extensive mobilization. It is necessary to consult the grass-roots officials, the masses and the management service objects to promote the interaction between the grass-roots and the headquarters, and to lay equal stress on management and service, so as to get the broadest possible support.

**7.1.4 Performance management is a competitive management of "pursuing excellence"**

The STA should conscientiously implement General Secretary Xi Jinping's important guiding principles of "working creatively through promoting innovation in ideas, means and grass-roots work", which is embodied in the fact that performance management should "emphasize on entrepreneurship, innovation and creation". We should adhere to the principle that "only the reformers advance, only the innovators are strong, only the reformers and innovators win", focus on the strategic objectives of performance, constantly expand the scope of vision, broaden working ideas, carry forward the spirit of entrepreneurship, highlight reform and innovation, pay attention to creative work, combine top-level design with grass-roots implementation, and combine breaking through with establishing logic system. We also incorporates and promotes the introduction, digestion, absorption and re-innovation and continue to promote performance management to a next level in a deeper, higher and newer realm.

### 7.1.5 Performance management is an aggressive management of "overcoming difficulties and forging ahead"

The STA should conscientiously implement General Secretary Xi Jinping's important guiding principles of "The reform is urgent and difficult. The heavier the task and the greater the difficulty, the more important advancing in the face of difficulties", which is embodied in the need for performance management to tackle difficulties. We should persist in carrying forward the spirit of never shying away from difficulties, never escaping responsibility and overcoming difficulties, "thinking from the worst and striving for the best", fully estimate the difficulties, and make up our minds that "as long as the direction is correct and of great significance, we should boldly try and break through", with the heroic spirit of "the Red Army facing down challenges on its march, braved ten thousand crags and torrents". We will continue to make new progress and achieve new results by overcoming one difficulty after another.

**7.1.6 Performance management is an upgrade management of "progressive development"**

The STA should conscientiously implement General Secretary Xi Jinping's important guiding principles of "striving to achieve the established goals with perseverance" and "making the institution more mature and well-defined is a dynamic process", which are embodied in the fact that performance management should be "able to advance, improve and make constant progress". Adhering to "steadfastly pushing forward, steadfastly reforming and steadfastly using", adopting the strategy of "first piloting, then pushing forward", and strengthening the concept of continuous improvement of "promoting performance management works with performance management philosophy", we can not only keep pace with the development of practice, but also keep pace with the times, and at the same time, we can do so in the spirit of self-revolution. It is not a temporary change in one thing, but a persistent change in everything to achieve smooth succession and upgrade.

### 7.1.7 Performance management is a reward and punishment management of "incentive and restraint"

The STA should conscientiously implement General Secretary Xi Jinping's important guiding principle of "being both strict and caring, and placing equal emphasis on providing incentives and imposing constraints", which is embodied in the fact that performance management should "incentivize behaviors that pursue high standards, punish behaviors that touch the bottom line, and lead the long-term development". We should adhere to the Party's management of officials, attach equal importance to both incentives and constraints, withstand pressure and link the results of performance evaluation with the selection and appointment of leading officials, the annual assessment of civil servants, commencement and awards and talent cultivation, strengthen incentives and constraints, and establish the performance orientation of "motivating pursuing high standard, punish touching the bottom standard, and leading long-term development". We should ensure that officials advocate practical work and maintain their vitality through the performance management of real and sustained efforts.

### 7.1.8 Performance management is a digital management empowered by science and technology

The STA should conscientiously implement General Secretary Xi Jinping's important guiding principle of "widely applying digital technology to public administration and services while promoting the digital and intelligent operation of the government", which is embodied in the fact that performance management should be "automatic data generalization and evaluation". Adhering to the principle of "science and technology is the first productive force" and making full use of modern information technology, we can not only improve information level through performance management, but also provide support for performance management through information construction, so as to promote more efficient and convenient performance management and more objective and fair performance evaluation, especially to adapt to the era of big data and strengthen the concept of digital performance. We should improve the level of quantitative computer examination with high-level information integration and give new momentum to performance management with digital transformation and intelligent upgrading.

**7.1.9 Performance management is a cultural management internalized in the mind**

The STA should conscientiously implement General Secretary Xi Jinping's important guiding principle that "confidence in one's culture, which is a broader, deeper, and more fundamental form of self-confidence, is the most essential, profound, and enduring source of strength", which is embodied in the fact that performance management should be full with care of humanism. We insist on cultivating a performance management culture with both characteristics of the department and the time in accordance with the idea of "keeping close to key nodes, advancing in an orderly manner, and gradually spreading out in an all-round way". We adopt an omnidirectional, multi-level, long-term and progressive strategy, which not only has a strong voice at key nodes, but also moistens things silently in daily life, so as to rally people's hearts and minds. Efforts should be made to pursue lofty ideals and conscious action of all departments at all levels to actively conduct performance management, so as to provide profound cultural support for its implementation.

**7.1.10 Performance management is a cognitive management of "strengthening understanding and conviction"**

The STA should conscientiously implement General Secretary Xi Jinping's important guiding principles that "theory comes from practice and is used to guide practice", "keenly understand the truth of Marxism and its innovative theories adapted to the Chinese context, and enhance the firmness of consciously implementing the Party's innovative theories", which are embodied in the fact that performance management should be based on the understanding of principle, theory and mechanism. We should understand and grasp the world outlook and methodology of Xi Jinping Thought on Socialism with Chinese Characteristics for a New Era, adhere to and apply the standpoints and methods that run through it, and guide the practice of performance management. We should strengthen theoretical thinking, achieve the unity of knowledge and practice, adhere to the "integration of learning, application and research", promote practice step by step, and deepen theoretical research. We must constantly boost confidence, reach a broad consensus, find solutions during encountering management problems, and promote the development of performance management in depth in the combination of theory and practice.

## 7.2 Future prospects

No performance management can be called the best, only better. Tax performance management has been implemented for nearly ten years, and has made hard-won achievements with the persistent pursuit of better and mature and well-defined on the road forever, meanwhile, there are still shortcomings in the innovation of theory, the scientificity of indicators, the comprehensiveness of evaluation, the maturity of technology and the depth of culture, which need to be further improved. The 20th National Congress of the Communist Party of China has made a comprehensive plan for the development of the Party and the state in the next five years and even until 2035, and the new journey has given a new mission of tax modernization. To further study and implement the guiding principles of the 20<sup>th</sup> National Congress of the Communist Party of China, to focus on building a modern socialist country in an all-round way, to unswervingly promote tax performance management, to ensure that the role of tax functions is fully played, and to serve Chinese modernization with tax modernization, we need to make sustained efforts from five further steps.

**7.2.1 Deepening the theoretical exploration of performance management: further highlighting the requirements of Chinese modernization**

The report of 20<sup>th</sup> National Congress of the Communist Party of China points out that, at the fundamental level, we owe the success of our Party and socialism with Chinese characteristics to the fact that Marxism works, particularly when it is adapted to the Chinese context and the needs of our times. The sound theoretical guidance of Marxism is the source from which our Party draws its firm belief and conviction and which enables our Party to seize the historical initiative. Xi Jinping Thought on Socialism with Chinese Characteristics

for a New Era is the Marxism of contemporary China and of
the 21st century. It embodies the best of the Chinese culture
and ethos in our times and represents a new breakthrough in
adapting Marxism to the Chinese context. The new era and
new journey put forward new questions and new requirements
for government governance. Only by adhering to emancipat-
ing the mind, seeking truth from facts, keeping pace with the
times and seeking truth and pragmatism, can we deeply grasp
the logical, historical and realistic inevitability of the development of performance management. Facing the future and
promoting the practice of tax performance management in
depth, we must consistently strengthen the scientific theory
armed with the Marxism adapted to the Chinese context and
the needs of our times. Guided by Xi Jinping Thought on Socialism with Chinese Characteristics for a New Era, we should
adhere to and make good use of the standpoints, viewpoints
and methods that run through it, base on the national condi-
tional, draw lessons from foreign countries and the history,
grasp the contemporary era, and further strengthen the Party's
overall leadership and highlight the political guidance from a

broad perspective of linking history with reality, linking inter-national and domestic, and combining theory with practice. The masses should judge the gains and losses of the work and test the effectiveness of the work in order to highlight the supremacy of the people. We implement the performance management model with Chinese characteristics in close con-nection with the national conditions and tax conditions to highlight self-confidence and self-reliance. We continuously improve the performance management system on the basis of persistence and inheritance to highlight integrity and innova-tion. We always focus on the new problems faced by practice, try to make new breakthroughs to highlight the problem ori-entation, and comprehensively consider organizational per-formance and individual performance. Tax performance man-agement stands at the forefront of government performance management and contributes tax wisdom to highlight the ser-vice of overall situation. It will contribute to speeding up the construction of national performance management system and promoting the construction of its discipline system, academic system and discourse system with Chinese characteristics and style.

**7.2.2 Strengthening the basic functions of performance management: further implementing the Party's organizational lines in the new era**

The report of the 20<sup>th</sup> National Congress of the Communist Party of China emphasizes that the Party's advantages and strength lie in its close-knit organizational system. Party organizations at all levels must perform the duties prescribed to them by the Party Constitution, implement the Party's lines, principles, policies and the Central Committee's decisions and plans, while attach importance to and strengthen the construction of staff team, which is our Party's fine tradition and basic experience. Focusing on building and strengthening the Party's ruling backbone, General Secretary Xi Jinping pioneered the Party's organizational lines in the new era, which calls for the integrated promotion of the "five systems" of quality training, character and ability, selection and appointment, rigorous management and positive incentives. Facing the future and promoting the practice of tax performance management in depth, we must consistently and conscientiously implement the Party's organizational lines in the new era. We should acquire a deep understanding of the decisive significance of the establishment of both Xi Jinping's core position on the Party Central Committee and in the Party as a whole and the guiding role of Xi Jinping Thought on Socialism with Chinese Characteristics for a New Era, and boost our consciousness of the need to maintain political integrity, think in big-picture terms, follow the leadership core, and keep in alignment with the central Party leadership. We should stay confident in the path, the theory, the system, and the culture of socialism with Chinese characteristics. We should firmly uphold Xi Jinping's core position on the Party Central Committee and in the Party as a whole and uphold the Central Committee's authority and its centralized, unified leadership. When formulating the strategic objectives of our departments or our business field, we should pay attention to developing a well-conceived approach to planning and advancing the endeavors on all fronts in a forward-looking and holistic manner, and constantly improving our political position and strategic thinking. We commit to build a contingent of tax officials who are politically competent, adapt to the requirements of the new era, and have the ability to lead and promote the taxation modernization. In the process of promoting tax modernization and serving Chinese modernization, we should give full play to the role of baton, vane and booster of performance management, promote unified will, unified action and concerted progress, and strive to build a well-off society in an all-round way. We encourage and guide tax authorities and tax officials at all levels to implement the decisions and deployment of the central government in a better state and a more practical style of work.

**7.2.3 Expanding the effectiveness of performance management practice: further promoting the high-quality development of tax work**

The report of the 20th National Congress of the Communist Party of China emphasizes that high-quality development is the primary task of building socialist modernization in an all-round way. New development concepts must be implemented comprehensively and accurately. A series of requirements are put forward for optimizing the tax structure, strengthening tax adjustment, improving the personal income tax system, and improving fiscal and taxation policies to support green development. Tax authorities are given higher standards and requirements for undertaking their missions and performing their duties. Promoting high-quality tax modernization with high-quality performance management is an inherent requirement. Facing the future and promoting the practice of tax performance management in depth, we must consistently give full play to the basic, pillar and supportive role of taxation in national governance. We further enhance the effectiveness of performance management in improving tax administration and collection and high-quality workforce, and scientifically formulate leading, comprehensive and key performance evaluation indicators around the strategic goal of serving Chinese modernization with tax modernization. We focus on fully leveraging, expanding and enhancing the role of taxation to create a more rigorous performance management closed-loop, highlight the implementation of responsibilities, and ensure the consistency of powers and responsibilities. Organizational performance is consistent with individual performance. We should improve the quality and efficiency of tax work, develop tax cause with higher quality, and enhance the efficiency and credibility of tax authorities.

### 7.2.4 Accelerating the technological upgrading of performance management: further improving the level of digitalization and intelligentization

The report of the 20$^{th}$ National Congress of the Communist Party of China calls for innovation to be at the core of Chinese modernization drive. In the era of big data, data is everywhere. Whoever owns data resources and makes the best use of them wins the future. Big data is the strategic resource of national governance system and governance modernization. Promoting the construction of digital government is an important measure to build a modern governance system. To a large extent, the governmental governance of information is the analysis, utilization and governance of data. Facing the future and promoting the practice of tax performance management in depth, we must consistently upgrade the level of digitalization and intelligentization. We should make full use of the Internet, big data, artificial intelligence and other technical means, and actively promote the integration of business and management to achieve digitalization and intelligentization. We should constantly strengthen the ability of automatic data generalization, transmission and evaluation for performance management, and coordinate task allocation, business process, post responsibility system and information system and integrate them into performance management, so as to improve the level of automatic evaluation and the quality and efficiency of performance management.

**7.2.5 Enhancing the value recognition of performance management: further cultivating endogenous and persistent motivation**

The report of the 20th National Congress of the Communist Party of China put forward that we should promote cultural confidence and strength and create new brilliance of socialist culture. Culture is the soul of a country and a nation. The prosperity of culture is the prosperity of the country, and the strength of culture is the strength of the nation. Only by sublimating the "hard measures" of the institution into the "soft power" of culture can any management mode play a more in-depth and lasting role. Further cultivating the performance

management culture of "internalized in the mind, external-
ized into practice and to honor commitment and take practical
actions" is the only way to promote the tax authorities at all
levels and the majority of tax officials to deepen their understanding of performance management, improve their awareness and then cohere their recognition. Facing the future and
promoting the practice of tax performance management in
depth, we must consistently put people first, cultivate people
with culture, and cultivate performance management culture.
Guided by the socialist core values, we should vigorously promote the spirit of China, disseminate the values of China and
rally the strength of China, promote the formation of ideological concepts, spiritual outlook, civilized customs and behav-
ioral norms that meet the requirements of the new era, and
inject solid foundation into the concepts, methods, measures
and means of performance management. It highlights respect-
ing, caring for, serving, supporting and leading people, and
does a good job in improving performance and telling good
performance stories. It constantly radiates a new atmosphere
of cohesion, consensus and kinetic energy.

责任编辑：刘志江　邓创业　卓　然　戚万迁
装帧设计：胡欣欣

**图书在版编目（CIP）数据**

中国税务绩效管理／国家税务总局课题组　著 . —北京：
　人民出版社，2023.8
ISBN 978－7－01－025811－9

I.①中…　II.①国…　III.①税收管理－研究－中国
　IV.① F812.423

中国国家版本馆 CIP 数据核字（2023）第 128637 号

**中国税务绩效管理**
ZHONGGUO SHUIWU JIXIAO GUANLI

国家税务总局课题组　著

**人民出版社** 出版发行
（100706　北京市东城区隆福寺街 99 号）

北京中科印刷有限公司印刷　新华书店经销

2023 年 8 月第 1 版　2023 年 8 月北京第 1 次印刷
开本：880 毫米 ×1230 毫米 1/32　印张：6
字数：96 千字

ISBN 978－7－01－025811－9　定价：42.00 元

邮购地址 100706　北京市东城区隆福寺街 99 号
人民东方图书销售中心　电话（010）65250042　65289539